D0147142

THE AGE OF NATIONALISM
The First Era of Global History

WORLD PERSPECTIVES

Volumes already published

BOARD OF EDITORS

of

WORLD PERSPECTIVES

Niels Bohr
Richard Courant
Hu Shih
Ernest Jackh
Robert M. MacIver
Jacques Maritain
J. Robert Oppenheimer
I. I. Rabi
Sarvepalli Radhakrishnan
Alexander Sachs

WORLD PERSPECTIVES · *Volume Twenty-eight*

Planned and Edited by RUTH NANDA ANSHEN

THE AGE OF NATIONALISM

The First Era of Global History

HANS KOHN

GREENWOOD PRESS, PUBLISHERS
WESTPORT, CONNECTICUT

PHILADELPHIA COLLEGE OF PHARMACY & SCIENCE
J.W. ENGLAND LIBRARY
RELEASED
4200 WOODLAND AVENUE
PHILADELPHIA, PA 19104-4491

2938363

Library of Congress Cataloging in Publication Data

Kohn, Hans, 1891-1971.
   The age of nationalism.

   Reprint of the 1st ed. published by Harper, New York,
which was issued as v. 28 of World perspectives.
   Includes index.
   1. History, Modern--20th century. 2. Nationalism--
History. I. Title.
[D445.K58 1976]   909.82   76-27696
ISBN 0-8371-9087-8

THE AGE OF NATIONALISM
Copyright © 1962 by Hans Kohn

All rights reserved.
No part of this book may be used or repro-
duced in any manner whatsoever without
written permission except in the case of
brief quotations embodied in critical articles
and   reviews.

Originally published in 1962 by Harper & Brothers, Publishers, New York

Reprinted with the permission of Harper & Row, Publishers, Inc.

Reprinted in 1976 by Greenwood Press
A division of Congressional Information Service
88 Post Road West, Westport, Connecticut 06881

Library of Congress Catalog Card Number 76-27696

ISBN 0-8371-9087-8

Printed in the United States of America

10 9 8 7 6 5 4 3 2

RELEASED

Contents

D
445
K79a

WORLD PERSPECTIVES

What This Series Means

It is the thesis of *World Perspectives* that man is in the process of developing a new consciousness which, in spite of his apparent spiritual and moral captivity, can eventually lift the human race above and beyond the fear, ignorance, and isolation which beset it today. It is to this nascent consciousness, to this concept of man born out of a universe perceived through a fresh vision of reality, that *World Perspectives* is dedicated.

Only those spiritual and intellectual leaders of our epoch who have a paternity in this extension of man's horizons are invited to participate in this Series: those who are aware of the truth that beyond the divisiveness among men there exists a primordial unitive power since we are all bound together by a common humanity more fundamental than any unity of dogma; those who recognize that the centrifugal force which has scattered and atomized mankind must be replaced by an integrating structure and process capable of bestowing meaning and purpose on existence; those who realize that science itself, when not inhibited by the limitations of its own methodology, when chastened and humbled, commits man to an indeterminate range of yet undreamed consequences that may flow from it.

This Series endeavors to point to a reality of which scientific theory has revealed only one aspect. It is the commitment to this reality that lends universal intent to a scientist's most original and solitary thought. By acknowledging this frankly we shall restore science to the great family of human aspirations by which men hope to fulfill themselves in the world community as thinking and sentient beings. For our problem is to discover a principle of differentiation and yet relationship lucid enough to justify and to purify scientific, philosophic and all other knowledge, both discursive and intuitive, by accepting their interdependence. This is the crisis in consciousness made articulate through the crisis in science. This is the new awakening.

Each volume presents the thought and belief of its author and points to the way in which religion, philosophy, art, science, economics, politics and history may constitute that form of human activity which takes the fullest and most precise account of variousness, possibility, complexity and difficulty. Thus World Perspectives endeavors to define that ecumenical power of the mind and heart which enables man through his mysterious greatness to re-create his life.

This Series is committed to a re-examination of all those sides of human endeavor which the specialist was taught to believe he could safely leave aside. It interprets present and past events impinging on human life in our growing World Age and envisages what man may yet attain when summoned by an unbending inner necessity to the quest of what is most exalted in him. Its purpose is to offer new vistas in terms of world and human development while refusing to betray the intimate correlation between universality and individuality, dynamics and form, freedom and destiny. Each author deals with the increasing realization that spirit and nature are not separate and apart; that intuition and reason must regain their importance as the means of perceiving and fusing inner being with outer reality.

World Perspectives endeavors to show that the conception of wholeness, unity, organism is a higher and more concrete conception than that of matter and energy. Thus an enlarged meaning of life, of biology, not as it is revealed in the test tube of the laboratory but as it is experienced within the organism of reality itself, is attempted in this Series. For the principle of life consists in the tension which connects spirit with the realm of matter. The element of life is dominant in the very texture of nature, thus rendering life, biology, a trans-empirical science. The laws of life have their origin beyond their mere physical manifestations and compel us to consider their spiritual source. In fact, the widening of the conceptual framework has not only served to restore order within the respective branches of knowledge, but has also disclosed analogies in man's position regarding the analysis and synthesis of experience in apparently separated domains of knowledge suggesting the possibility of an ever more embracing objective description of the meaning of life.

Knowledge, it is shown in these books, no longer consists in a manipulation of man and nature as opposite forces, nor in the reduction of data to mere statistical order, but is a means of liberating mankind from the destructive power of fear, pointing the way toward the goal of the rehabilitation of the human will and the rebirth of faith and confidence in the human person. The works published also endeavor to reveal that the cry for patterns, systems and authorities is growing less insistent as the desire grows stronger in both East and West for the recovery of a dignity, integrity and self-realization which are the inalienable rights of man who may now guide change by means of conscious purpose in the light of rational experience.

Other vital questions explored relate to problems of international understanding as well as to problems dealing with prejudice and the resultant tensions and antagonisms. The growing perception and responsibility of our World Age point to the new reality that the individual person and the collective person supplement and integrate each other; that the thrall of totalitarianism of both left and right has been shaken in the universal desire to recapture the authority of truth and human totality. Mankind can finally place its trust not in a proletarian authoritarianism, not in a secularized humanism, both of which have betrayed the spiritual property right of history, but in a sacramental brotherhood and in the unity of knowledge. This new consciousness has created a widening of human horizons beyond every parochialism, and a revolution in human thought comparable to the basic assumption, among the ancient Greeks, of the sovereignty of reason; corresponding to the great effulgence of the moral conscience articulated by the Hebrew prophets; analogous to the fundamental assertions of Christianity; or to the beginning of a new scientific era, the era of the science of dynamics, the experimental foundations of which were laid by Galileo in the Renaissance.

An important effort of this Series is to re-examine the contradictory meanings and applications which are given today to such terms as democracy, freedom, justice, love, peace, brotherhood and God. The purpose of such inquiries is to clear the way for the foundation of a genuine *world* history not in terms of nation or race or culture but in terms of man in relation to God, to himself, his fellow man and the universe, that reach beyond immediate self-interest. For the meaning of the World Age consists in respecting man's hopes and dreams which lead to a deeper understanding of the basic values of all peoples.

World Perspectives is planned to gain insight into the meaning of man, who not only is determined by history but who also determines history. History is to be understood as concerned not only with the life of man on this planet but as including also such cosmic influences as interpenetrate our human world. This generation is discovering that history does not conform to the social optimism of modern civilization and that the organization of human communities and the establishment of freedom and peace are not only intellectual achievements but spiritual and moral achievements as well, demanding a cherishing of the wholeness of human personality, the "unmediated wholeness of feeling and thought," and constituting a never-ending challenge to man, emerging from the abyss of meaninglessness and suffering, to be renewed and replenished in the totality of his life.

Justice itself, which has been "in a state of pilgrimage and crucifixion" and now is being slowly liberated from the grip of social and political demonologies in the East as well as in the West, begins to question its own premises. The modern revolutionary movements which have challenged the sacred institutions of society by protecting social injustice in the name of social justice are examined and re-evaluated.

In the light of this, we have no choice but to admit that the unfreedom against which freedom is measured must be retained with it, namely, that the aspect of truth out of which the night view appears to emerge, the darkness of our time, is as little abandonable as is man's subjective advance. Thus the two sources of man's consciousness are inseparable, not as dead but as living and complementary, an aspect of that "principle of complementarity" through which Niels Bohr has sought to unite the quantum and the wave, both of which constitute the very fabric of life's radiant energy.

There is in mankind today a counterforce to the sterility and danger of a quantitative, anonymous mass culture, a new, if sometimes imperceptible, spiritual sense of convergence toward world unity on the basis of the sacredness of each human person and respect for the plurality of cultures. There is a growing awareness that equality may not be evaluated in mere numerical terms but is proportionate and analogical in its reality. For when equality is equated with interchangeability, individuality is negated and the human person extinguished.

We stand at the brink of an age of a world in which human life presses forward to actualize new forms. The false separation of man and nature, of time and space, of freedom and security, is acknowledged and we are faced with a new vision of man in his organic unity and of history offering a richness and diversity of quality and majesty of scope hitherto unprecedented. In relating the accumulated wisdom of man's spirit to the new reality of the World Age, in articulating its thought and belief, *World Perspectives* seeks to encourage a renaissance of hope in society and of pride in man's decision as to what his destiny will be.

World Perspectives is committed to the recognition that all great changes are preceded by a vigorous intellectual re-evaluation and reorganization. Our authors are aware that the sin of *hubris* may be avoided by showing that the creative process itself is not a free activity if by free we mean arbitrary, or unrelated to cosmic law. For the creative process in the human mind, the developmental process in organic nature and the basic laws of the inorganic realm may be but varied expressions of a universal formative process. Thus *World Perspectives* hopes to show that although the present apocalyptic period is one of exceptional tensions, there is also at work an exceptional movement toward a compensating unity which refuses to violate the ultimate moral power at work in the universe, that very power upon which all human effort must at last depend. In this way we may come to understand that there exists an inherent independence of spiritual and mental growth which though conditioned by circumstances is never determined by circumstances. In this way the great plethora of human knowledge may be correlated with an insight into the nature of human nature by being attuned to the wide and deep range of human thought and human experience.

In spite of the infinite obligation of men and in spite of their finite power, in spite of the intransigence of nationalisms, and in spite of the homelessness of moral passions rendered ineffectual by the scientific outlook, beneath the apparent turmoil and upheaval of the present, and out of the transformations of this dynamic period with the unfolding of a world consciousness, the purpose of *World Perspectives* is to help quicken the "unshaken heart of well-rounded truth" and interpret the significant elements of the World Age now taking shape out of the core of that undimmed continuity of the creative process which restores man to mankind while deepening and enhancing his communion with the universe.

RUTH NANDA ANSHEN

New York, 1962

FOREWORD

It is widely accepted in the Western world to speak of the decades after 1914 and especially after 1933 as an age of apocalyptic anxiety and of exceptional tensions. Such periods have been known throughout human history. The present period is distinguished from preceding ones not by its intensity of uncertainty or fear, but by its global character. All preceding history has been parochial history. In the middle of the twentieth century mankind has entered the first stage of global history.

It is at the same time characteristic for this new age of history that I hesitate to use the term world history. "World" has been used so far indiscriminately to mean on the one hand the whole created universe, the cosmos, and on the other hand the earth and earthly concerns, which in reality are only a tiny part of the universe, though the part most closely related to man. We are on the threshold of an age in which man will acquire new spatial experiences and concerns and in which the word "world" will gain a new meaning sharply distinguished from the history and condition of man on our earth. Therefore I prefer the term "global history."

The following essay deals with events of the second third of the twentieth century. It views them in the perspective of preceding history, not primarily as an age of political and social upheaval but as one of changes in the mind and attitude of men. The views expressed here involve also a new periodization of world or global history. The analysis presented is based upon previous studies. To allow the flow of the argument to go forward in the brief compass of this book, I have referred in footnotes to other writings for the documentation of the point of view put forth here.

The new historical era upon which we are entering opens, as did all its predecessors, as a time of great travail and trouble which burden the spirit of man. Yet the historian of today may view the future with cautious hopefulness, a hopefulness aware of the limitations of man and the unpredictability of history. The author who is approaching his seventieth year and who in the span of his grown-up life has witnessed two world wars and two world revolutions is no *laudator temporis acti*. The life of the large majority of men before 1914 was as little a sweet life as that of the multitudes before 1789. *La douceur de la vie* was enjoyed by a very small privileged minority before 1914. Since then many more people have attained a life of growing comfort and a feeling of human dignity and social responsibility than any one thought possible in 1914.

The complexity and ambivalence of all history may be seen in the fact that this broadening of the bases for a more dignified human life occurred in Europe after 1789 under the overall concept of an age of nationalism, and occurs outside Europe in the twentieth century under similar guiding stars. In this age for the first time a common attitude includes peoples and civilizations all over the globe, and this under the sign of nationalism. Therefore this new age may be called the age of pan-nationalism. Yet nationalism, in Europe as elsewhere, has carried not only a hope and a promise but also a grave threat to the growing unity of mankind and to the rational freedom of man. The garb of nationalism clothes on the one hand the human aspirations for equality and dignity and on the other hand the passion for power over others, the most permanent and fateful feature and agent of human history. In the age of nationalism, nationality has been the vehicle of much domestic progress, but to quote Lord Acton, "The process of civilization depends on transcending nationality." The new era of global history, which I call the age of pan-nationalism, will find its ultimate justification in transcending itself in an international global order for which it creates the premise.

HANS KOHN

New York, January 1962

"The recent Past contains the key to the present time. All forms of thought that influence it come before us in their turn, and we have to describe the ruling currents, to interpret the sovereign forces, that still govern and divide the world. . . .

"By Universal History I understand that which is distinct from the combined history of all countries, which is not a rope of sand, but a continuous development, and is not a burden on the memory, but an illumination of the soul. It moves in a succession to which the nations are subsidiary. Their story will be told, not for their own sake, but in reference and subordination to a higher series, according to the time and the degree in which they contribute to the common fortune of mankind."

Lord Acton as Editor of the
Cambridge Modern History, 1898

"These propensities . . . . will furnish fresh weapons to each succeeding generation that struggles in favor of the liberty of mankind. Let us, then, look forward to the future with that salutary fear which makes men keep watch and ward for freedom, not with that faint and idle terror which depresses and enervates the heart."

Tocqueville, Democracy in America

PART ONE

THE AGE OF NATIONALISM
THE TRANSFORMATION OF EUROPE

"May it [the Declaration of Independence] be to the world, what I believe it will be—to some parts sooner, to others later, but finally to all—the signal of arousing men to burst the chains under which monkish ignorance and superstition has persuaded them to bind themselves, and to assume the blessings and security of self-government."

Thomas Jefferson, letter,
June 24, 1826

I

THE FRENCH Revolution of 1789 marked a turning point in Western history. In the beginning it seemed that the new and deeper renaissance to which all Europe aspired in the second half of the eighteenth century was being realized in France. Contact with the ideas of the French Revolution awakened the dormant political life and thought on the European continent, especially in Germany and Italy. The cult of liberty, the aspiration toward nationhood one and indivisible, the longing for a new national cohesion and a new national spirit, the idea of a state rooted in popular consent and enthusiasm and supported by the active participation of the people—all these concepts were eagerly learned from France.

But in France itself the emphasis rapidly shifted between 1789 and 1793. The tyrant to be fought was no longer the domestic oppressor but the foreign enemy; the liberty worshipped was not so much individual freedom from a strong authoritarian government but national independence and power. It was in that form— as nationalism and passion for power—more than in the form of liberalism and enlightened humanism that the French Revolution exercised its influence on the European continent. The new nationalism aroused by the French Revolution abroad turned against France. Vincenzo Cuoco recognized it in his "Saggio Storico" of the Neapolitan revolution of 1799. "Strange character of all the peoples of this earth! The desire to give them an exaggerated liberty awakens in them a longing for freedom from the liberators themselves."

The French Revolution started in order to realize the new concept of limited government introduced by the English and American Revolutions. In August, 1789, the Declaration of the Rights of Man expressed the ideas of liberty and of equality in the abolition of all traditional privileges and discriminations. Equality remained an ideal under the republic and under Napoleon, but liberty lost itself almost immediately in the exaltation of national glory which found its chief representation in the army. The army

3

saved the Republic in 1793. But even after the security of France had been restored and an end put to the terror, the leaders of the new regime did not press for peace. Though the people longed for a new ease of life, they could be swayed without difficulty to pursue the road to glory. Robespierre prepared the way for Napoleon, the ideologue for the soldier, the virtue of the revolutionary zealot for the cold Machiavellianism of power.

The enthusiasm for a militant expansionist nationalism and the accompanying diminution of constitutional liberty distinguished the French Revolution from those in the English-speaking countries. The latter, especially the Anglo-American one, carried a universal message, too, but this message played only a subordinate role. The revolutions of 1640 and 1776 occurred at the outskirts of the civilized world and dedicated themselves mainly to immediate and national concerns. The Revolution of 1789 happened in the heartland of European civilization. It aroused a passionate enthusiasm throughout the whole Western world. It was regarded, and not only by the French, as a means of the regeneration of mankind. Paris became the New Jerusalem. The revolution "created an atmosphere of missionary fervor and, indeed, assumed all the aspects of a religious revival. . . . This strange religion has overrun the whole [Western] world with its apostles, militants, and martyrs." The French Revolution could influence the whole Western world because men's minds were prepared for the reception of the new ideas. What was wholly novel in the situation was that so many nations "should have simultaneously reached a stage in their development" which enabled the ideology of the revolution to be readily accepted.[1]

The French Revolution had a twofold impact on the Western world. In countries with old-established concepts of liberty, with local self-government and limitation of power, it strengthened

[1] Alexis de Tocqueville, *The Old Regime and the French Revolution* (Doubleday Anchor Books, 1955), p. 13. See about this readiness for revolution at the end of the eighteenth century, this search for regeneration through nationalism and democracy in the Western world, Hans Kohn, *The Idea of Nationalism. A Study in Its Origins and Background* (7th printing, New York: Macmillan, 1958), chs. VI to VIII; R. R. Palmer, *The Age of the Democratic Revolution: The Challenge* (Princeton University Press, 1959).

democracy. That was the case in the United States, in Britain, in Switzerland and in those small European lands which on the whole followed the pattern of English nationalism—Scandinavia and the Netherlands. In other countries the French Revolution aroused a militant nationalism. The spirit of the French army set a model. It put General Buonaparte in command of the nation in 1799. Constitutions on paper followed each other and representative institutions endowed with little power provided a democratic façade. Thus the French did not develop the respect for constitutions and for parliamentary bodies characteristic of the British and the Americans. French and Continental nationalism in general inherited the spirit of the absolutist monarchy with its fear of self-government and its drive towards centralization. In his study of "The Old Regime and the French Revolution" Tocqueville has shown—and his thesis has been confirmed by many scholars since—that the Revolution and Napoleon continued the growing interference of the monarchy with the whole life of France. "Under the old regime, as nowadays, there was in France no township . . . however small, no hospital, factory, convent, or college which had the right to manage its own affairs as it thought fit. . . . Then, as today, the central power held all Frenchmen in tutelage." Though the French overthrew despotism in 1789, their background "made them less qualified than perhaps any other nation to replace it by a stable government and a healthy freedom under the sovereignty of law." One hundred and twenty years later, the French and other Continental European nations had not yet reached the goal of stable freedom and respect for legality.[2]

In the centralization of power and in his ambitions, Napoleon I went far beyond the monarchy. He superimposed upon French nationalism the heritage of the Roman imperial idea. As the alleged heir of Charlemagne he united France, Western Germany,

[2] Tocqueville, op. cit., pp. 51, 120. Tocqueville wrote this in 1856, at the height of the regime of Napoleon III. It was a time when in the pursuit of national glory, to quote Tocqueville, "no one in France set any store on liberty." Twenty years later liberty was revived in France, but it was later repeatedly threatened, in the Dreyfus affair, under Pétain and by the war against Algerian liberty. See Hans Kohn, Making of the Modern French Mind (New York: Van Nostrand, 1955).

Italy and the Low Countries in his empire. When he annexed the Papal States on May 17, 1809, he did so on the strength of the theory that the secular domain of the pope had been a fief of Charlemagne, "Empereur des Français et notre auguste prédécesseur." Napoleon wished to go farther than Charlemagne and Rome. "We owe it to Napoleon," Nietzsche predicted, "that several war-like centuries, which have not had their like in past history, may now follow one another—in short, that we have entered upon the classical age of war, at the same time scientific and popular." Nietzsche's expectation of "several war-like centuries" may be wrong; more correct seems his forecast that "inescapably, hesitatingly, terrible like fate, the great task and question approaches: how should the earth as a whole be administered? and to what end should man as a whole—no longer a people or a race—be raised and bred?" To that end, Napoleon, as Nietzsche said, "wanted one Europe, which was to be the mistress of the world." This dream of European domination of the world, today gone forever, obsessed, in a perverted form, Hitler. But the unity of Europe, a new kind of holy or rather unholy Roman Empire, could not be achieved even for the purpose of world domination. Napoleon and Hitler, and all similar would-be unifiers of Europe or the world for the sake of dominion or leadership, by necessity aroused the resistance of nationalism. For the protection of their liberty, tranquillity, and diversity, the other peoples united against them and overthrew the "new order" of conquest and uniformity. Global domination by any one nation, ideology or leader has become impossible in the Age of Nationalism.

One of Napoleon's liberal critics, Benjamin Constant, clearly recognized the reason why all revivals of the Roman spirit were doomed in modern times. War was the instrument of the past, he wrote, commerce, that of enlightened civilization. "Commerce is an attempt to receive by agreement what one no longer hopes to conquer by force. A man who would always be the strongest would never think of commerce. It is experience which, in demonstrating to him that war—this is to say, the employment of his force against that of another—is exposed to various resistances and checks, leads him to have recourse to commerce—that is to say, to a more pleasant and certain way of compelling the interests of others to consent to what accommodates his own interest. . . .

Carthage, fighting with Rome in ancient times, had to succumb; it had the force of circumstances against it. But if the fight between Rome and Carthage were taking place today, Carthage would have the universe on its side. She would have had for allies the true morals and spirit of the world."[3]

II

THE CONGRESS of Vienna, at the end of the Napoleonic wars, attempted to restore prenationalist Europe. "For a long time now," Metternich wrote to Wellington in 1824, "Europe has had for me the quality of a fatherland." For more than forty years, until Napoleon III and Otto von Bismarck used the means of militant nationalism in the service of their power ambitions, Europe went through a period of international peace. There was no trace of armament races and no concentration on progress in military technology. This peace, however, was one of self-satisfied complacency bent upon the preservation of the status quo. Yet the semi-mystical awe with which the divine right dynasties had been regarded began to lose its luster through the Napoleonic wars, though it survived among the German upper and middle classes and perhaps among the Russian peasantry until the beginning of the twentieth century. Count Bismarck in Germany and Count Cavour in Italy helped to undermine the principle of dynastic legitimacy by their unceremonious ejection of ancient dynasties. Behind the aristocratic façade of life, the slow but deep democratic and social revolution which was expressed in the ideas

[3] Henri Benjamin Constant, *De l'esprit de conquête et de l'usurpation dans leurs rapports avec la civilisation européenne* (1813) (Paris: Bernard Grasset, 1918), ch. II: "Du caractère des nations modernes relativement à la guerre," pp. 12, 14. Constant characterized Napoleon's regime in a way which foreshadowed the nationalist and socialist revolutions of a later time. Its representatives "regarded weakness as ignoble, laws as superfluous subtleties, and despised parliamentary forms for their allegedly unbearable slowness. They preferred rapid and trenchant decisions as in war, and thought unanimity of opinion as essential as in an army. Opposition they regarded as disorder, critical reasoning as revolt, the courts as military tribunals, the judges as soldiers who must execute the orders of authority, those who were suspect or accused as if they were enemies and convicted criminals, and the judgments of the courts as battles in the state of war into which they transformed government." *Ibid.*, p. 25.

of 1789 permeated after 1815 to a varying degree first the educated classes and then the masses in the various European countries, finally even in Russia and the Near East.

At the end of February, 1848, the revolution erupted again in France and the Second Republic was established. This time the events affected all of central Europe with an unexpected speed. The renewed revolution carried everywhere the twofold heritage of 1789—liberalism and nationalism. Again, as it did half a century before, nationalism proved stronger than liberalism. As far as the latter survived on the European continent, it put itself into the service of a militant nationalism. In France herself, the overwhelming majority of the people were lured by Napoleonic ideas. The Second Republic ended in the military dictatorship of the Second Empire. "There is nothing older in the world," Edgar Quinet wrote then, "than people who acclaim success, who welcome in the evening what they cursed in the morning. It is useless to create a new word for that—authoritarian democracy—as if any authority placed in the stead of law were not the very negation of democracy. I have so often seen democracy and liberty taken in by cheap promises of establishing freedom sometime in the future, after [national] strength and union have done their work. But meanwhile the masses have become impenetrable to the considerations of [universally valid] justice and liberty."

The militant nationalism which was to carry Napoleon III to power found its spokesman in Jules Michelet, the historian of France and of the French Revolution, who occupied at the Collège de France the chair of Histoire et Morale. His book Le Peuple (1846) was a call to France to unite for the necessary strength of carrying through her mission as "the glorious pilot of mankind's ship." He foresaw critical times, a threat to France and to civilization from west and from east, from England and Russia. France could trust only in her own strength, based upon her unity, her consciousness of a great historical mission, the discarding of her pusillanimous and worn-out ruling class, the bourgeoisie. In the people of France Michelet found still surviving "the sentiment of military honor always renewed by our heroic legend, the invisible spirit of the heroes of our wars, the wind of the old flag. . . . On the day of the supreme battle between civilization and barbarism (who knows whether it will not be tomorrow?) the Judge must find the young soldiers [of France] irreproachable, their swords clean, their bayonets shining. Whenever I see them pass, my heart is moved; here alone force and idea, valor and right, which elsewhere are separated, go hand in hand. If the world can be saved by war you alone will save it. Sacred bayonets of France, take care that nothing will darken that light which shines over you and which no eye can bear."[4]

Napoleon III used and abused the faith in the army and in France's destiny of which Michelet had so praisingly spoken. Soon Michelet and other leading French intellectuals repudiated Napoleon III.[5] Less courageous in the cause of liberalism were the intellectuals throughout central Europe. There in 1848–49 the conflicting ambitions of the various nationalisms defeated the hope of liberalism and of international peace and enabled semi-absolutist conservative monarchies to survive. This nationalist fervor continued to plague central Europe after 1918, the year of the fall of the monarchies. In fact, the nationalism of the peoples showed itself more ardent and aggressive, behind the façade of republican or democratic constitutions, than that of the monarchs.

III

IN THE period between the Napoleonic wars and 1848, nationalism had slowly come to dominate the public mind of the educated classes in Germany and Italy and among the other central European peoples. At the beginning of the nineteenth century

[4] See Hans Kohn, Prophets and Peoples. Studies in Nineteenth-Century Nationalism (4th printing, New York: Macmillan, 1957), ch. II.

[5] Tocqueville repudiated Napoleon III most strongly. But he, too, showed himself, before 1848 as a deputy in the French Chamber, a strong nationalist and imperialist, concerned with France's glory abroad. He opposed his friend Claude de Corcelle, when the latter insisted that France had given in Algeria "an example of an insensate return to the most barbarous deeds." But in 1847, after a second visit to Algiers, Tocqueville recorded the failure of the "regime of the saber." He criticized the "weight of double centralization at Algiers and at Paris." A commission of the Chamber summed up in 1847 the results of French control of Algeria: "We have rendered Musselman society more miserable, more disorganized, more ignorant, and more barbarous than it was before it knew us." See Mary Lawlor, S. N. D., Alexis de Tocqueville in the Chamber of Deputies: His Views on Foreign and Colonial Policy (Washington: Catholic University of America, 1959).

cosmopolitanism (*Weltbürgertum*) and love of peace were still dominant, above all in Germany. Kant and Goethe adhered to it throughout their lives. Many German intellectuals praised Napoleon, and when they turned from him it was not because he was an "alien" but because he had betrayed the promise of cosmopolitan peace. But by the end of the Napoleonic Wars many intellectuals upheld the claims of race and history over those of cosmopolitan life and individual liberty.

"In itself every nationality (*Stamm*) is a completely closed and rounded whole," Josef Görres, the foremost German political journalist of the "War of Liberation" against Napoleon, wrote, "a common tie of blood relationship unites all its members; all . . . must be of one mind (*Gesinnung*) and must stick together like one man. This instinctive urge which binds all members into a whole is the law of nature which takes precedence before all artificial contracts. . . . The voice of nature in ourselves warns us and points to the chasm between us and the alien." But even while Görres expressed this view, history and blood were not strong enough to overcome the inclinations of the present and of the free spirit. Many continued to prefer liberty to the alleged call of the blood. The German-speaking Swiss and Alsatians who until the seventeenth century had formed part of the German Empire and whom Görres called "home" into the new German Reich insisted on their freedom to decide on their separateness. In the United States a nation was born out of many bloods and pasts through the beneficial assimilation of individuals and whole ethnic groups. Even in Germany Görres had to complain that very many longed for the return of the French. The years of alien influence left in some German hearts a preference for the French order of things to the blessings which national honor brought.

German scholars of the early nineteenth century continued to warn against emphasis on unity and power. The historian Arnold Herman Ludwig Heeren praised in 1817 the weak and loose German Confederation as the *Friedensstaat von Europa*, Europe's guarantee of peace. Should Germany become a united nation-state, situated in the very heart of Europe, a compact mass disposing of great resources in manpower, natural and industrial products, Heeren warned, it could hardly resist the temptation of using its geographic and strategic advantages to become the *Kriegsstaat von Europa*, Europe's warrior state. Heeren not only rejected German national unity: he was one of the first continental writers to foresee that the European balance of power was not a permanent basis of history, as the European politicians assumed until 1939, but that it would give way to a world balance of power, with the stage of history quickly broadening beyond Europe, soon to encompass the whole earth. The new era of sea power and world order, he believed, would usher in a happier future for mankind. Another German historian of this period, Michael Alexander Lips, a staunch liberal, hostile to all remnants of feudalism and all economic controls, suggested in 1814 the formation of a liberal European union. The German philosopher Karl Christian Friedrich Krause, who exercised a great influence on Spanish thought, published in 1814 the draft for the constitution of a European federation which he considered a regional system within a future federation of mankind. For three months he edited a *Tagblatt des Menschheitlebens*, the first daily dedicated to the cause of global government.

But after 1830 the majority of European continental liberals grew more nationalist than liberal. The emphasis on national unity and power, on the maximation of national territory to its greatest extent reached in history, the appeal to alleged rights based on the "ancestral" past destroyed the cosmopolitan and humanitarian concerns for one's fellow men of other nationalities. Strategic reasons of national survival or security and moral reasons of cultural superiority or economic productivity were adduced to justify territorial claims and privileges of status against other nationalities—German against Polish, Polish and Russian against Ukrainian, Magyars against Slovaks, French against Algerian, English against Irish, to name only a few examples. Looking on the European scene of 1848, John Stuart Mill wrote in the *Westminster Review* in April, 1849 that nationalism makes men indifferent to the rights and interest "of any portion of the human species, save that which is called by the same name and speaks the same language as themselves." He complained that "in the backward parts of Europe and even (where better things might have been expected) in Germany, the sentiment of nationality so far outweighs the love of liberty that the people are willing to abet their rulers in crushing the liberty and independence of any people not of their race or language."[6]

IV

NATIONALISM as it was realized all over Europe in the century following 1848 did not fulfill the hopes expressed by Jefferson in the letter which he wrote in 1826 as one of the sages of the age of Enlightenment. As he foresaw, the Declaration of Independence which he had drafted fifty years before helped to spark the the movements for independence all over the globe—in some parts of the globe sooner, in other later, but finally in all—and inspired the peoples to seek the "blessings" of self-government. But the new nationalism did not resemble the Anglo-American prototype. Nationalism—like all historical mass-sentiments, f.i. religion—has its good and its evil aspects. The various nationalisms differ therein according to the political ideas and traditions which they embody, to the memories and hopes they evoke, to their attitude toward neighbors and the international community, to the degree of their self-centeredness and claim of exclusivity. In its beginning, nationalism bursts the fetters of tradition (what Jefferson called "monkish superstition"), of an obsolete and restrictive social order, and fills the hearts of its followers with the sense of human dignity, with the pride and satisfaction of participation in history, in the management of one's own affairs. This feeling of liberation was as characteristic of the early nationalism in nineteenth-century Europe as it is today in Asia and Africa.

Nationalism has its divisive aspects, too. It can become self-centered and its group egotism has infinitely more dangerous implications, practically and morally, than individual egotism. Nationality is only a fragment of humanity which, however, in the Age of Nationalism tends to regard itself as the whole. A universal religion which insists on the oneness of mankind and the supremacy of the individual over all ties of race and descent, or the

[6] See Hans Kohn, *The Twentieth Century*. New Edition (New York: Macmillan, 1957), pp. 3–31, and J. L. Talmon, *Political Messianism. The Romantic Phase* (New York: Frederick A. Praeger, 1960), pp. 229–292, 472–515.

humanitarian rationalism of the age of Enlightenment in which Jefferson lived and the French Revolution started, can prevent nationalism from degenerating into a supreme and exclusive claim upon man's loyalty. But a nationalism not tempered by regard for the overruling values of humanity and the rights of other peoples, grows morally sterile and politically dangerous to civil liberty and peace. Then nothing remains but the nation, which has become the one and the whole, the supreme guide of man's action and thought. Such a nationalism especially when it is based upon racial or religious uniformity or exclusivity produces, if it disposes of military strength and a militant spirit, a grave threat to its neighbors, and in any case a source of spiritual decay to its own members. A nationalism which claims sanction by the will of God or History, by religion or by a semireligious ideology, leads to the dangerous assumption of the position of a "unique" people, a chosen people.

There are other far-reaching differences between the various nationalisms. In the North Atlantic countries, in the age of Enlightenment, nationalism was generally conceived as based not upon biological determinism, but upon the free will of the individuals; it tended toward the recognition of diversity and the harmonization of conflicting or differing interests and religious and ethnic traditions. Such was also the case in Switzerland. Swiss nationalism, like that of the United States, rejected the concept of race or common descent as the basis of a state; it rested instead on a spiritual decision: on the right and liberty of the individual human personality, which was recognized as the strongest creative force in the cultural and moral realm.[7]

Like the Swiss nation, but in a very different way, the United States does not base its nationalism on common descent or on a common religion. Nor does it accept a romantic rootedness in the soil, a *Verbundenheit mit dem Boden*, to use the German term, as one of its foundations. From its beginning Anglo-America has

---

[7] These words were used in the message of the Swiss Federal Council to the nation in December 1938. See Hans Kohn, *Nationalism and Liberty. The Swiss Example* (London: Allen & Unwin, and New York: Macmillan, 1956), p. 129. Similarly Lord Acton pleaded in his essay "Nationality" (1862) for states containing various ethnic and religious groups on the footing of equality as a safeguard of liberty. See Hans Kohn, *Nationalism, Its Meaning and History* (Princeton: Van Nostrand, 1955), pp. 121–125.

shown a unique liberty and spontaneous diversity in its religious life, differing therein from all other Western countries at the beginning of the nineteenth century. No one religion could be identified with Anglo-America, no one religion inspired its desire for independence. The old Goethe, a warm admirer of the United States, was deeply impressed by this—as by other—aspects of American tolerance. "In New York," he noted, "there are ninety different Christian denominations, each one of which worships its God and master in its own way without feeling disturbed by the fact. We must advance to a similar freedom in science and scholarship. We talk a lot about liberalism, and yet, with us, every one wishes to hinder his fellow man from thinking and expressing himself in his own way."

The unique geographic and social mobility and the ever new frontiers of life in the United States have prevented that attachment to rootedness in the soil and to ancestor worship which transforms so much of nationalism elsewhere into a cult of chthonic gods. The American nation, when it was established, lacked even a name of its own which would point to its territory or ancestry. "America" is more than the name of a nation, it stands for about twenty nations from the Arctic to Cape Horn, and "The United States" is less than the name of a nation; like the similar "The United Nations," it was not found to designate a national soil but the goal of unity in diversity, of the harmonization of conflicting and varying interests by the power of an idea. As little as "soil," "blood" has been the cementing tie of American nationality. Even before the United States was constituted as a nation, the melting pot had begun to function. The Frenchman Crèvecœur, who lived in North America as a farmer in Pennsylvania from 1759 to 1790, wrote "of that strange mixture of blood, which you will find in no other country." Since then the most various ethnic strains have entered into the texture of the nation. They changed it physically but not in its substance. They were received and assimilated into the new alma mater and nourished and transformed by it.

The Americans constituted themselves as a nation not on the basis of some peculiar and exclusive biological or traditional characteristics but on the basis of a universal idea. They started as the heirs and guardians of the English tradition of individual liberty and representative government. "In political theory, in political practice," the American historian Carl Becker wrote, "the American Revolution drew its inspiration from the [English] parliamentary struggle of the seventeenth century. The philosophy of the Declaration [of Independence] was . . . not new, but good old English doctrine newly formulated to meet a present emergency."[8] But to become a nation of its own the United States had to do more than to adapt the English tradition of liberty to a special emergency. The Declaration universalized and thereby transcended the English tradition of liberty as it had developed from older roots in the two English Revolutions of the seventeenth century. What had been the historical birthright of Englishmen became in America, under the influence of the eighteenth-century Enlightenment, a universal message, the birthright of man.

The American Whigs originally regarded the liberty for which they started to fight as an inheritance; they wished to conserve, as James Otis expressed it, "the British constitution, the most free one on earth." But by their struggle they did not only preserve it, they transformed it into a new idea which found its embodiment in the Constitution and its Bill of Rights, documents which have shown, through almost two centuries of great changes, a rare persistency and vitality. The Constitution which the young nation adopted in 1789 is the oldest constitution in force. During all this time it has been the supreme symbol and manifestation of the American idea, which, out of English roots, has become in principle a universal idea. Destined, in theory, for all men who wished to accept it, it has proven itself endowed with a unique assimilative power: the United States was the only nation in which large-scale immigration has played a decisive role and in which many millions of immigrants of the most varied backgrounds and former national allegiances have been willingly transformed and integrated into a national tradition and civilization, which in many instances had no common roots with their own.

The liberal and universal character of American nationalism

[8] Carl Becker, *The Declaration of Independence* (New York: Harcourt, Brace, 1922), pp. 79, 231. See on the problems of American nationalism Hans Kohn, *American Nationalism* (New York: Macmillan, 1957), and his *The Idea of Nationalism*, ch. VI.

marks it as representative of one of the possible developments of nationalism. Another element which distinguished American nationalism from the beginning was its federal character. At the time of the founding of the Republic and in the first decades of the nineteenth century it was frequently assumed—among others by Rousseau—that small states alone could afford to function as democratic republics, but that large territories with the accompanying diversity of populations could develop in an orderly way only as monarchies or aristocracies. Federalism, from the township upwards, pointed the road to reconciling freedom and order, diversity and unity. On the other hand Tocqueville saw in a federal constitution the best safeguard for avoiding or mitigating the tyranny which a majority might exercise in democratic states. Through the local self-government inherent in the federal system people can even in very large nations participate in the process of government and acquire the experience, and be inspired with the feeling, which they need in order to govern well. In the United States "the Constitution has not destroyed the individuality of the states, and all communities, of whatever nature they may be, are impelled by secret instinct towards independence."

It was different in the centralized nations of Europe. Tocqueville did not expect them to imitate the American institutions, "for I am well aware of the influence which the nature of a country and its political antecedents exercise upon its political constitution; and I should regard it as a great misfortune for mankind if liberty were to exist all over the world under the same features. But I am of the opinion that if we do not succeed in gradually introducing democratic institutions into France, if we despair of imparting to all the citizens those ideas and sentiments which first prepare them for freedom and afterwards allow them to enjoy it, there will be no independence at all, either for the middle classes or for the nobility, for the poor or for the rich, but an equal tyranny over all; and I foresee that if the peaceable dominion of the majority is not founded among us in time, we shall sooner or later fall under the unlimited authority of a single man."[9] French nationalism in the 130 years since Tocqueville

[9] Alexis de Tocqueville, *Democracy in America* (New York: Knopf, 1945), I, 330. On p. 425 Tocqueville wrote: "America is a land of wonders, in which everything is in constant motion and every change seems an improvement.

wrote these lines has often threatened to succumb to this danger which he foresaw, but the liberal spirit of 1789 has so far always reasserted itself; the traditions of liberty, on the other hand, were too weak in Germany or Russia to prevent nationalism there from degenerating into an absolutism which bore out Tocqueville's words that "if absolute power were re-established among the democratic nations of Europe, I am persuaded that it would assume a new form and appear under features unknown to our fathers."[10]

V

OTHER forms of nationalism look above all to ancestry and the past. In the Old Testament tradition these nationalisms often are based upon historical claims sanctified or glorified by appeals to the plans of Divinity or to promises bestowed by the God of History. The conviction of being a people chosen by God or History has, in ancient and again in modern times, sometimes even fused with a biological belief in the value of common descent and racial purity, in the embodiment of the true faith or the true civilization in people of one "seed" or "blood." Understandably such a people thanks God for having singled it out in such a way and tends to regard itself as representing an especially noble type. In 1853 Count Arthur de Gobineau identified this noble race with the Germans or the Aryans, and proclaimed that racial purity guarantees the eternity of a people whereas intermarriage leads to degeneration and carries the seed of death with it. According to him true civilization can exist only where the Aryan race predominates. When on the other hand the Aryan blood becomes exhausted, stagnation supervenes.

Gobineau's theory of the foundation of a modern nation on racial purity found few adherents in France. Leading French historians like Michelet and Renan stressed racial intermingling as the fertile basis of French nationalism and as the indispensable foundation of a liberal policy. In 1863, ten years after the publi-

The idea of novelty is there indissolubly connected with the idea of amelioration. No natural boundary seems to be set to the efforts of man; and in his eyes what is not yet done is only what he has not yet attempted to do!"

[10] *Ibid.*, p. 326.

cation of Gobineau's work, Louis Joly wrote in his "Du Principe des Nationalités" that stress on ancestors was contrary to the principles of 1789. "The idea of an association of men which is not constituted on the sympathies and hatreds stemming from common descent is superior to one based upon the recognition of these 'natural' sympathies and hatreds. The fusion of races, as it happened in France, Britain and the United States, is one of the great beneficial factors of history. The leading powers in the world are the very ones where the various nationalities and racial strains which entered into their formation have been extinguished as far as possible and have left few traces."

Tocqueville, Gobineau's personal friend, sharply rejected his racial theory as "fatalistic" (man determined by his ancestry) and "materialistic" (this determination based upon physiological factors). But his main objection was moral and historical. "Don't you see how inherent in your doctrine are all the evils produced by permanent inequality: pride, violence, the scorn of one's fellow men, tyranny and abjection in every one of their forms? . . . You chose precisely the thesis which, to me, has always seemed the most dangerous one for our times. [This is even more applicable to the twentieth than to the nineteenth century. H. K.]. . . . The last [eighteenth] century had an exaggerated . . . trust in the control which men and peoples were supposed to have of their own destinies. It was the error of those times; a noble error, after all; it may have led to many follies, but it also produced great things, compared to which we shall seem quite small in the eyes of posterity. The weary aftermath of revolution, the weakening of passions, the miscarriage of so many generous ideas and of so many great hopes have now led us to the opposite extreme.[11] After

[11] Tocqueville wrote in the period of disillusionment after the failure of the hopes of 1848 and the triumph of conservatism and reaction. In another letter, of October 11, 1853, he described the panicky conservatism prevailing in the French middle class, a conservatism which in the name of order, religion, decency and property had helped Napoleon III establish his regime: "The socialists have produced, and are still producing, so much fear that even the corner grocer does not want to hear anything discussed that is unorthodox; he keeps repeating that the people should be kept within bounds to impede the abolition of Property and Family, and to prevent them from ransacking his grocery. There is now little taste for freedom of thought; it is enough for an idea to seem dangerous and a sort of universal silence is drawn

having felt ourselves capable of transforming ourselves, we now feel incapable of informing ourselves." Gobineau's emphasis on ancestry, blood and inheritance, Tocqueville believed, strengthened the conservative tendencies and the lassitude of a generation faced by great tasks of future human cooperation and improvement.[12]

Tocqueville predicted that Gobineau's ideas might fall upon a fertile soil in Germany. "Alone in Europe, the Germans possess the particular talent of becoming impassioned with what they take as abstract truths, without considering their practical consequences; they may furnish you with a truly favorable audience whose opinions will sooner or later re-echo in France, for nowadays the whole divided world has become one." Tocqueville's prediction regarding the Germans proved true. Richard Wagner became Gobineau's admiring follower. He even exaggerated the French count's belief in the unique creativeness of the Germanic race; in his eyes racial purity and the influence of ancestry on man's thought and personality forbade the possibility and desirability of the assimilation of the Jews in their European homelands. He denied that Jews could become creative in German or other European languages "alien" to them. "Our whole European art and civilization have remained to the Jew as a foreign tongue . . . at most the homeless wight has been a cold, nay more, a hostile on-looker. . . . Alien and apathetic stands the educated Jew in the midst of a society he does not understand," Wagner wrote, "with whose tastes and aspirations he does not sympathize, whose history and evolution have always been indifferent to him." Thus the racial theory of nationalism proclaimed one of the most radical antitheses to the creed of liberalism and of the Enlightenment, of 1776 and 1789, namely that Jews could become "creative" only in their "own" land and their "own" language, the land and language of their distant "ancestors."

Nationalism in the Western world was in its beginning, in the eighteenth century, and perhaps down to 1848, a movement of emancipation—emancipation from the closed world of the past,

---

around it. There is not enough faith, not enough passion, not enough vitality to combat such ideas; instead they are shunned. . . ."

[12] See letters of 11 Oct., 17 Nov. and 20 Dec. 1853; 30 July 1856; 14 Jan. 1857 in Tocqueville's *The European Revolution and Correspondence with Gobineau*, ed. by John Lukacs (Doubleday Anchor Books, 1959).

the promise of an open future, in which tolerance and liberalism would integrate various, formerly separated, religious and ethnic groups, classes and castes. After 1848 the policy of liberalism was largely abandoned on the European continent. Historical pride and exaggerated nationalism set up people against people. National self-assertiveness of one people aroused similar reactions in its neighbors. From 1848, which was greeted as a year of hope and peace, until 1945, the "utopian" expectations of the peaceful co-operation of free men faded into a "realistic" national self-assertiveness at the expense of other nations and into preparedness for combat. Modern Europe and Western civilization were weakened, and finally in danger of collapse, not because the ideas which animated their rise in the late seventeenth and in the eighteenth centuries were wrong but because they were, in deeds even more than in words, abandoned or repudiated.

One of the few Europeans who resisted this development was Jean Jaurès. As philosopher, historian, journalist and socialist leader, he remained faithful to the traditions of 1789 and 1848. There was nothing narrow or dogmatic about him. It was characteristic of him that he saw the "universe as an immense, a vague, aspiration toward order, beauty, liberty," and that he called the daily newspaper which he founded in 1904 l'Humanité. Again it was characteristic that he fell a victim to the passions leading Europe into the abyss of the war. On July 31, 1914 he was assassinated by a nationalist. His life and hopes were destroyed by the mentality against which he had warned throughout his mature years. At the time of a momentary relaxation of international tensions, which closed the second Morocco crisis between Germany and France at the end of 1911, he demanded, in a speech before the Chamber of Deputies on December 20, that the French should not only carry out wide and generous policies in favor of the Moroccans but in favor of all countries and resist all nationalist temptations. "We remain surrounded by an atmosphere of suspicion and defiance from which, it seems to me, the clouds of war may descend upon us at any minute. As far as it is our responsibility, the responsibility of a great people, we must constantly apply ourselves to dissipate this atmosphere of defiance and to combat the causes of the renewed danger of conflict. It is our

primary duty to reject the pessimism and the fatalism of those
who say that war is inevitable."

"The present-day armies of each nation represent entire peoples,
as in the times of primitive barbarism," Jaurès went on, "but this
time they would be let loose amidst all the complexity and wealth
of human civilization. Each of these nations would employ the
instruments of terrifying destruction created by modern science.
Do not imagine that it will be a short war, consisting of a few
thunderbolts and flashes of lightning. . . . This terrible spectacle
will overstimulate all human passions." As a socialist, Jaurès
pleaded for an evolutionary development of society towards
greater social justice. A war, he warned, would unleash the destructive hatreds "which have hitherto accompanied all great movements for social reform throughout history. It is in the fever of
wars that passions for social reform are aroused to a paroxysm of
violence." Therefore conservatives should desire peace, for once
peace is broken in modern times the forces of chaos will be let
loose.

Jaurès credited three active forces with "working for peace today." The first of these was obviously the international organization of the working class. The second was the cooperation of
industrial and financial capitalism across national frontiers. "This
is the beginning of capitalist solidarity, which can be dangerous if
it is not . . . controlled by public opinion or by independent
governments. If, however, it is controlled, enlightened, and
watched over by great, independent and proud nations, it might
help bring peace to the world in times of instability."

This evaluation of international capitalism by a socialist leader
testified to the independence of his mind and the breadth of his
views. More surprising was the third force which Jaurès found
working for peace in the world, "Anglo-Saxon America, reborn
from the old puritan ideals. Gentlemen, we do not know the great
American people or the American conscience. We only see their
dollar-mindedness; we only see men obsessed by millions, by business, and by gold. There are signs which indicate that the
Americans have overcome their crisis. . . . Therefore we find
in America a revival of idealism which is not only a surface manifestation, since it digs beneath the dollar era and the period of

mercantile materialism to find America's puritan soul which has its roots in the enthusiasm of the Biblical prophets, and which, in its manner, has dreamed of a free and just society. . . . Should Europe be foolish enough to divide and tear itself apart tomorrow, this great enlightened American idealism would shame it with its proposals for arbitration."[13]

French nationalism, after the fall of the Napoleonic Empire, was turned against Britain and demanded revenge for Waterloo. When Michelet traveled in 1834 in England, he was deeply mortified by his recognition that the collapse of Britain, which he had foreseen and desired, might after all not happen. All the monuments of London revolted him by evoking in him the memory of "Waterloo, Waterloo, partout!" England, Michelet was convinced, "covering her sordid interests with political fictions in mendacious language in which she herself does not believe, has long been working for the ruin of France, using in the eighteenth century the genius of France—Voltaire, Montesquieu, Mirabeau— to deceive her. . . . Strange and capricious insolence!" he exclaimed. "To wish to domineer over a country which in spite of its paltry government . . . was captivating the world by the power of its mind! . . . I should like to see an English idea! A great and fruitful moral idea! England never had, nor will she ever have, any great moralist or jurist."[14]

Yet a self-critical recognition of the greater strength of English liberty and political maturity was not missing. After the downfall of the Napoleonic Empire, Saint-Simon in an essay on "The Reorganization of European Society" suggested that Britain and France should unite for preserving peace and securing liberty, to form as the leading liberal parliamentary states the nucleus of a European federation. He demanded an Anglo-French parliament, composed of two-thirds English and one-third French deputies because the French needed "the guidance of the experienced

[13] OEuvres de Jean Jaurès, Pour la Paix, Europe Incertaine (Paris: Rieder, 1934), pp. 423–434, also in Jaurès, Pages Choisies (Paris: Rieder, 1922), pp. 434–42.

[14] Michelet and most French intellectuals of the time were pro-German and anti-British. The French government, on the other hand, sought peace and cooperation with Britain. That explains partly the widespread contempt for the pacific or "paltry" policy of Louis Philippe.

English." France had need of British support, because it was embarking upon parliamentary government and faced the domestic threats of authoritarian rule on the one hand and of an extravagant liberty on the other. Over half a century later Renan pleaded for a close perpetual alliance of Britain, France and Germany which alone could integrate Russia into Europe, and mitigate Prussia's militarism in the interest of the Germans. "Let Prussia take heed. Her extreme policy can engage her in a series of complications from which it will not be easy to disentangle herself. A penetrating eye could perhaps perceive the formation of future coalitions. The wise friends of Prussia will tell her, not as a threat but as a warning: *væ victoribus*, woe to the victors."

While German nationalism, from its rise in 1806, was anti-French, French nationalism turned against Germany only after 1870. It was motivated by resentment over the violence which the Germans had done to Alsace on the strength of historical rights and for the sake of ingathering all Germans into the German nation-state. This Franco-German tension, which turned Europe after Bismarck's triumph into an armed camp, formed also part of a hegemonical struggle for the control of the Continent, with Russia looming large in the background. In the Revolution and under Napoleon the French had succumbed to the *hubris* of leadership and aroused coalitions against them; in 1871 Renan foresaw a similar future for Germany. Pleading with both nations to abandon their hegemonical struggle, he warned that Germany's territorial claims based on ancient history or racial ties would ultimately ruin Germany. "You have erected in the world a standard of ethnographical and archeological policy instead of a liberal policy; this policy will be fatal to you. . . . How can you believe that the Slavs will not do to you what you are doing to others?" The German claims of 1871 and the Slav claims of 1945 disregarded the rights of the living populations in the name of historical rights. "How much better it would have been for you," Renan warned the Germans in 1871, "if you could have reserved for that day," the coming of which he foresaw, "the right to appeal to reason, to morality, to friendships based on common principles." In the name of these principles Renan wished to unite a liberal Britain, a liberal France, and a liberal Germany. "Let all of us together take up the great and true problems, the social problems of finding a rational organization for mankind which would be as just as is humanly possible."[15]

VI

EXCESSIVE and militant nationalism was not confined to Germany and France. It was virulent in almost all European countries. To the historian it sounds rather strange when he hears Europeans complain about the "immaturity" or "extremism" of nationalism in Asia or Africa today. There is little found in Asian or African nationalism today which has not a close parallel in, or has not been surpassed by, European attitudes in the late nineteenth or early twentieth century. The anti-British resentment in Ireland and the violent forms of its expression or the anti-Hapsburg sentiment among the Czechs at least equaled even the anticolonialism to be found in non-European lands. Nor was this bitter hostility confined to nations of different racial origin or linguistic family. Serbs and Bulgars—both people of Slavic origin, of Greek Orthodox faith and of a long common history of subjection to Turkish rule—faced each other throughout their existence as modern independent nations in implacable enmity and fought several wars over frontiers and over the territory of Macedonia to which both of them laid "historical" claims. The Slavic Russians and Poles were enemies for three hundred years. They were only united in their oppression of a third Slavic people, the Ukrainians.

The great Russian liberal, Alexander Herzen, pleaded from his exile in London with the Polish exiles, as he pleaded with his fellow Russians, to recognize the Ukrainians' right to their own freedom. "If the Ukraine recalls," he wrote in 1859, "on the one hand, all the Muscovite oppression, the serfdom, recruiting, absence of rights, the corruption and the knout; if, on the other hand, she does not forget how she fared under the Polish Rzeczpospolita with her soldiers, gentlemen, and crown officials—what,

---

[15] See Ernest Renan, La Réforme Intellectuelle et Morale, ed. by P. E. Chavret (Cambridge University Press, 1950), pp. 79–104, 119–127, and Recollections of My Youth, tr. by C. B. Pitman (London: Chapman & Hall, 1883), pp. xiii–xxi.

then, if she wants to be neither Polish nor Russian. In my opinion this question is easily settled. The Ukraine should be recognized as a free and independent country. Among us exiles . . . there cannot be, there must not be, any question as to the ownership of this or the other piece of settled land. In Ukraine there live human beings . . . who have not been so completely broken by their government and their landowners that they have lost all their national feelings. . . . Would it be a step toward their liberation, if after taking off their Muscovite chains, one were to tell them that they must belong to Poland? Let us untie their hands and loosen their tongues, that their speech may be altogether free and that they may speak their mind. . . . If they are wise, they will offer us their hand as brotherly allies, independent of both of us."[16]

Herzen wrote this a century ago; half a century later, after World War I and the downfall of the Russian empire, the Ukrainians continued to be denied the right of a free decision. They remained divided among, and subject to, "more highly developed," more state-conscious nations—Russians and Poles above all, but also Czechs and Rumanians. They were granted some autonomy within the Union of Soviet Socialist Republics, into which the Russian empire was transformed, and in which they were all united after World War II; but Poland denied her numerous and, thanks to their former Austrian citizenship, nationally developed Ukrainians the autonomy, which the victorious Allied Powers had promised them in 1919; even the meager minority rights for the use of the Ukrainian language, granted by the Polish Diet in 1924, the Polish administration refused to apply. The relatively liberal and law-abiding policy of the Austrian monarchy, which had been developing in the non-Hungarian parts of the Hapsburg empire after 1867, was replaced in most of the new states emerging from the First World War by an illiberal nationality policy in which the power of the state was put, in the name of nationalism, into the service of the dominant ethnic group. Instead of binational or constitutionally multi-ethnic states,

[16] See Hans Kohn, *The Mind of Modern Russia. Historical and Political Thought of Russia's Great Age* (New Brunswick, New Jersey: Rutgers University Press, 1955), pp. 175 ff. See there also Vladimir Solovev's brilliant criticism of Russian Slavophile nationalism, pp. 214 ff.

the ideal of a pure nation-state was proclaimed. Poland was to be as Polish and Rumanian as Rumanian as France was French. This attempt to apply Western European concepts to central-eastern and southern Europe, where historically and sociologically different ethnic conditions prevailed, undermined all over this region the promise of democracy, which the victory of 1918 seemed to carry.

The almost unexpected victory of 1918, achieved in the name of democracy by the temporarily and superficially united efforts of Britain, France and the United States, saved Lenin's regime in Russia from the imposition of the treaty of Brest-Litovsk and from further German conquests eastward; it promised central-eastern and southern Europe, from Germany to Bulgaria, from Latvia to Rumania, from Portugal and Spain to Greece, an era of democracy, of respect for the liberty and dignity of men of all classes, religions and ethnic groups, and for the reign of law under representative forms of government. In that sense the settlement of 1919 appeared as the reversal of the Viennese settlement of 1815. It was hoped that in the course of a century the fundamental attitudes of modern Western civilization had been adopted and taken root all over Europe. But that was not the case. The heritage of the humanitarian reforms and aspirations of the eighteenth and early nineteenth century was, often haughtily, abandoned.[17]

Less than twenty years after the end of World War I authoritarian dictatorships covered southern and central-eastern Europe, from the Estado Novo of March 19, 1933 under Dr. Antonio de Oliveira Salazar in Portugal and the Third Greece of August 4, 1936 under General Joannes Metaxas to the regime of Karlis Ulmanis, established on May 16, 1934 in Latvia. Fascism as an exaggerated self-centered form of nationalism prevailed almost everywhere, though sometimes in disguised form. But even where it did not replace democratic institutions, democracy was vitiated by the state acting as the agent of a favored ethnic group, religious community or class to the detriment and often humiliation of

[17] The chief example for this haughty rejection of modern Western civilization was of course Germany, a country where Western liberalism and humanism seemed more deeply rooted than in the Balkans or the Iberian peninsula. The reasons why this was not so are discussed in my *The Mind of Germany* (New York: Charles Scribner's Sons, 1960).

others. Nationalism in northwestern Europe and in North America meant, at least in theory, the emancipation of *all* peoples and groups as equal partners in a common state. With its spread to other parts of Europe it has been often debased into an instrument of domination of one nationality over others, which were regarded as not being of the nationality "owning" the state. While they themselves were "oppressed," the various nationalities appealed to the "natural" right of national self-determination. They announced that after the gaining of their national goals they would not do to others what they had rejected with bitter moral indignation when done to themselves. Reality proved almost always different. The former "oppressed" ones became sometimes worse "oppressors," not only of their own former "oppressors" but of "innocent" third peoples. A "historical" excuse for it was easily found and supported by scholars and glorified by poets. The recognition of the equality of all human beings, and their right to emancipation, promised by the democratic revolution in the Atlantic world at the end of the eighteenth century, was more often in deeds than in words repudiated. Nationalism became the self-centered demand for one's own emancipation, not the promise of a universal emancipation.

This fundamental change in the temper of nationalism was not clearly seen even at the beginning of the twentieth century. Theodore Roosevelt firmly believed that "Europe must be reconstructed on the basis of the principle of nationalities." From it he expected the coming of an era of peace. "The Austro-Hungarian and the Turkish Empire must be broken up if we intend to make the world even moderately safe for democracy," he wrote in words which many readers today may ascribe to Woodrow Wilson rather than to his great predecessor and opponent. "There must be a revived Poland, taking in all Poles of Austria, Prussia and Russia; a greater Bohemia, taking in Moravia and the Slovaks; a great Jugo-slav community including Serbia, Croatia, Bosnia and Hercegovina, while the Rumanians in Hungary should become part of Rumania and the Italians in Austria part of Italy. The Turk must be driven from Europe and Christian and Arab freed. Only in this manner can we do justice to the subject peoples tyrannized by the Germans, Magyars and Turks. Only in this way can we remove the menace of German aggression which has become the haunting night-mare for all civilizations, especially in the case of the small well-behaved liberty-loving peoples."[18]

Roosevelt, the typical optimist of the late nineteenth century, saw only one side of the picture. He did not realize that Yugoslav and Italian aspirations would be difficult to reconcile; that Arab lands liberated from the Turks would be partitioned among the British, the French and the Zionists; that the "small" peoples loved liberty more for themselves than for their neighbors, and that they were definitely not "well-behaved." The menace of German (and of Russian) aggression was not removed but increased as the result of the dissolution of the Austrian monarchy and the creation of many jealous and self-centered new states between the two giant nations. Fifteen years later German (and then Russian) aggression was to become again, and in a much intensified form, the haunting nightmare which it had been in the later nineteenth and the early twentieth centuries. The war of 1914 and even the victory of the Western democracies did not bring peace and did not assure the survival of Western civilization. On the contrary, the war and its outcome lessened and destroyed the faith in the future of democracy, not only in the defeated nations and in the new nations, but even in the ranks of the victors themselves. Democracy which had been rising since the eighteenth century and which seemingly was riding the crest of the wave in 1918, found itself twenty years later rapidly receding. Many questioned then whether modern Western civilization would survive.

[18] See David H. Burton, "Theodore Roosevelt: Confident Imperialist," *The Review of Politics*, vol. 23 (July, 1961), pp. 356–377; *The Works of Theodore Roosevelt*, Memorial Edition, New York 1922–26, XXI, 409.

PART TWO

THE COURSE OF WESTERN CIVILIZATION
THE NORTH ATLANTIC COMMUNITY

"I am myself by inclination a seeker after truth. I feel a consuming thirst for knowledge and a restless passion to advance in it, as well as satisfaction in every forward step. There was a time when I thought that this alone could constitute the honor of mankind, and I despised the common man who knows nothing. Rousseau set me right. This blind prejudice vanished; I learned to respect human nature, and I should consider myself far more useless than the ordinary working-man if I did not believe that this view could give worth to all others to establish the rights of man."

Immanuel Kant

I

MODERN Western civilization differs from older and contemporary dogmatic and authoritarian ways of life—in the broad sense of the word, including religions, ideologies and social political structures—by its critical and practical approach. All others have stressed uniformity and have called upon, or forced, their adherents to follow an unequivocal path of life, the only one which promises salvation. Western civilization, on the other hand, emphasizes diversity or, to quote from John Stuart Mill's *Autobiography*, "the importance, to man and society . . . of giving full freedom to human nature to expand itself in innumerable and conflicting directions."

Modern Western civilization is not identical with Greco-Roman civilization, with Europe or the Occident or with the Judeo-Christian tradition. Modern Western civilization arose in northwestern Europe in the seventeenth and eighteenth centuries. It was a new and revolutionary civilization, based upon the belief in the equal rights of all, irrespective of religion, ancestry or class; upon the concern for the dignity and humanity of every individual; and upon the right to intellectual and political opposition and criticism. Such conditions did not exist in Greece or Rome, in Judaism or Christianity, or in any European country before the eighteenth century.

Though modern civilization originated in northwestern Europe, it cannot be defined in a geographic way. Europe is a geographic term, not a cultural entity. Throughout history, from antiquity to the present day, its cultural configuration has been changing. Some European areas have not accepted or do not presently accept modern Western civilization. In the early spring of 1941, by far the greatest part of Europe—under the then apparently closely allied dictatorships of Stalin, Hitler, Mussolini and Franco—was confidently waging war on modern Western civilization and all its fundamental ideas. Nor is modern Western civilization identical with the Hellenic and Roman heritage. During many centuries this heritage was more faithfully and diligently preserved and developed in Byzantium and in Islam than

31

in the West. Nor can modern civilization be identified with Christianity, which is a universal religion, destined for all men and all civilizations. There are Christian communities of very ancient lineage, like the Ethiopian, which form no part of modern civilization, a civilization often sharply rejected in Orthodox, deeply Christian Russia and in Catholic, deeply Christian Spain.

In recent times Western civilization has been treated by its enemies as "senescent" or "obsolete." On this point the Russian Slavophiles and the Russian Marxists, Oswald Spengler and the Fascists have been in agreement. But seen in a historical perspective, Western civilization, as the term is used here, is not only very young but endowed with a vitality and a dynamism possessed by no previous civilization. The obituaries written by a fashionable *Kulturpessimismus* are, to say the least, premature.

The Occidental civilization of medieval Roman Christianity was historically connected with the Greco-Roman civilization of antiquity and yet fundamentally different from it. In the same way, modern civilization when it arose grew out of that civilization which has developed from the time of Charlemagne to the seventeenth century, and yet it was, in its feeling of life, as different from the older civilization as the latter was from Periclean Athens or Augustan Rome. The two older civilizations—the Greco-Roman and the Western or Latin Christian—were both based on the Mediterranean. Slowly between the fifteenth and the seventeenth century, the center of gravity shifted from there to the North Atlantic. In the period from 1470 to 1500 around 10,000 books were printed in Europe. Of them about half were printed in Italy—2,835 in Venice alone—while during the same thirty years only 130 books were printed in London and 7 in Oxford. Around the year 1500 Europeans discovered the earth, the first step toward the present global age. Portuguese and Spaniards took the lead in this great enterprise. For a brief moment it seemed as if the South Atlantic would hold a decisive place in a new phase of medieval Christian civilization. But Portugal and Spain quickly spent themselves. Too deeply bound up with the past, they lost touch with the new world of thought and enterprise which arose a century later around the North Atlantic. To this day Spain and Portugal have remained "underdeveloped" countries, a modern concept which gained validity only with the dynamism and the revolutionary *élan* which the new North Atlantic civilization introduced.

In 1519 Charles, King of Spain, became Roman Emperor and in his service Ferdinand Magellan set out on the first circumnavigation of the globe. In 1571 the Spanish fleet defeated that of Islam with whom Christianity had for more than nine hundred years contested the control of the Mediterranean. In that century, its Golden Century, Spain was the champion of the medieval unity of the Church, of the spirit of the Crusades, and of the Roman imperial idea. But in the following decades, England which like Spain had been a European borderland, even more backward and poor, became, together with Holland, the home of the intellectual, political and social revolutions, with which modern civilization started. From there it radiated to North America and to the European continent. England's rise marked the dawn of the North Atlantic era. A new period of history began, which was to become, in the course of two centuries, the first global era uniting all of mankind in intercourse and cross fertilization.[1]

II

MODERN civilization which originated in seventeenth-century England and Holland represents the greatest all-encompassing

[1] The outward decline of Spain began in 1588 and ended in 1898, with the loss of Cuba, Puerto Rico and the Philippines, the last remnants of the world empire. In both cases Spain faced the leading representative of that modern civilization which it rejected and despised. Anatole France has described the impression made by the news of the defeat of the Spanish fleet in 1898 in an aristocratic French family which was saddened by the vision "of a fleet blessed by the Pope, flying the flag of the Catholic King, carrying at the prow of its ships the name of the Virgin and of the Saints . . . disabled, battered, sunk by the guns of these merchants of hogs and manufacturers of sewing machines, heretics without kings, without an aristocracy, without a past, without a fatherland, without an army." In Spain, the generation of 1898, stung by the defeat and the corruption and backwardness which the defeat revealed, started a short period of searching self-criticism about Spain's relationship to modern civilization, similar to the great debate conducted in nineteenth-century Russia. But it all ended, at least for the time being, in the triumph of the old forces under Generalissimo Franco. Typically one of the leading spokesmen of the generation of 1898, Ramiro de Maeztu, ultimately defended in his *Defensa de la Hispanidad* (1934) the traditional Hispanophile values. See on the whole movement Luis Granjel, *Panorama de la Generación del 98* (Madrid: Ed. Guadarrama, 1960).

revolution in the conditions of human life and society. Its various strains are intimately interwoven and cannot be separated. When some of them are singled out in the following lines, their interdependence should not be forgotten. The new attitudes continued and at the same time transformed the heritage of the past. Greek intellectual curiosity, its attempt to replace magic by reason, helped to create the new spirit of science. It became the basis of an all-pervasive world-image. The new attitude stressed the practical applicability of science in order to alleviate human drudgery and suffering. Science acquired social significance; it became the most powerful instrument for raising the dignity and establishing the equality of all individuals. It gave rise to an optimistic belief in man's latent possibilities and accordingly in his right to be treated with respect.

Francis Bacon thought himself the first to point the way to a new use of science. According to him its aim was the good of society, "the relief of man's estate." He protested against Aristotle because "he had been incapable of doing anything for the welfare of mankind." In Bacon's attitude a utilitarian and experimental practical realism, a faith in a universal, rational morality, enhancing the dignity of man, and a desire for power over nature were combined with the fascination of the pioneering towards unknown frontiers. In his *New Atlantis* (1626) he wrote, "The end of our foundation is the knowledge of causes and secret motions of things, and the enlarging of the bounds of human empire, to the effecting of all things possible." About a decade later Descartes insisted in his *Discours sur la Méthode* that the place of scholastic philosophy should be taken by "a practical philosophy, through which, by understanding the force and action [of natural phenomena] as well as we understand the diverse trades of our artisans, we could employ them in like manner for all their proper purposes, and thereby become the very masters and possessors of nature." The Royal Society of London for the Improving of Natural Knowledge was recognized as the center of experimental research in western Europe. Voltaire in France, Benjamin Franklin in North America, became apostles of this new spirit of technological inventiveness, which later on ushered in the dynamic industrial revolutions from the steam engine to the electronic devices and made possible new living standards for men everywhere, an entirely un-Greek development out of Greek roots.

Another modern attitude was derived from the Roman tradition of law, without, however, accepting its authoritarian spirit or its cruelty towards human life and suffering. While insisting upon the rule and impartial majesty of law—a rational and universally applicable law, before which all men are equal—modern civilization filled the tradition of law with a new humane concern for, and with the intent of protecting, individual liberty against governmental authority. It replaced in Western lands the traditional adoration of power, which has, however, remained characteristic of central and eastern Europe even in modern times, with a distrust of the possible abuses of power and authority, and made vigilance against such abuses a feature of its governmental institutions and traditions. That was the great work performed by the English people in the seventeenth century. In the same revolutionary period Milton and Locke called for a latitude of tolerance, of freedom of thought and expression unknown before in Western history. This new spirit made the growth of an open and tolerant pluralistic society possible; the right to liberty and diversity was soon codified in the several bills of rights. A new critical and adventurous spirit created a society open to everything human, to all new ideas, a society which, in spite of its national organization, was of a basically cosmopolitan character. This open society for the first time allowed and promoted social and geographic mobility and opened new possibilities for the development of the abilities of all men.

With modern technology the need for unifying organization grew. The centralizing tendency was a necessity in view of shrinking distances and rapid population growth but it contained dangerous implications which had to be countered, in the interest of individuality and diversity, by a vigorous affirmation of the right to local self-government in order to balance the excessive concentration of authority in the hands of the state or of powerful corporate groups. Such a concentration of power and guidance in the state, at the expense of individual initiative and voluntary associations, has been traditionally accepted even in modern times in central and eastern Europe; recently the North Atlantic area, too, has witnessed a similar trend to extend the administrative powers and functions of the state into all realms of society, "tending toward a wide measure of politicisation of social, economic, and cultural life, not in the name of power but in that of progress, welfare and devotion to the common man." In the middle of the nineteenth century, Ralph Waldo Emerson and John Stuart Mill warned against these trends; they recalled that modern civilization means more than efficiency in promoting technology and welfare, it means a fundamental regard for individual liberty and diversity. The modern free state, a development of the seventeenth and eighteenth centuries, must remain inherently an open and pluralist society. "Its power will be limited by associations whose plurality of claims upon their members is the measure of their members' freedom from any monopoly of power in society."[2] The more technology and organization tend toward centralization of authority, the greater is the need, in advanced modern societies, to insist on the freedom of the individual and of association, on checks and balances in the government, on federalism and autonomy in local administration.

Modern civilization broke with all previous attitudes in its respect for manual labor and for the dignity of man engaged in practical work. "There is a radical incompatibility," Plato wrote in his *Republic*, "between the exercise of a manual profession and the rights of citizenship." This attitude survived in the European aristocratic tradition and was reversed only in modern civilization. The latter resumed and deepened the protest of the Biblical prophets against oppression of the weak and disinherited, a protest which was alive in the early Christian community. The sense of social responsibility in modern civilization has its historical root in the prophetic respect for the dignity of every individual. But the modern social consciousness alone has regarded for the last two hundred years a steady progressive amelioration of living conditions as a duty incumbent upon society. This social consciousness was not concerned only with material improvements; it brought about an unprecedented refinement of mores, a rapid mitigation of the barbaric penal laws and punishments prevailing from Biblical times until the European eighteenth century, and ushered in a struggle against slavery and all forms of human degradation.

Until the eighteenth century, men everywhere—in Europe, Asia

[2] See Robert A. Nisbet, *The Quest for Community. A Study in the Ethics of Order and Freedom* (New York: Oxford University Press, 1953).

and Africa—were brutalized. In Roman times they enjoyed the horrors of the circus. In the Middle Ages and down to the seventeenth century they flocked to all spectacles of cruel executions, whippings and torture. Compassion with suffering seemed as alien to the large majority of people everywhere as was the concern for the well-being and dignity of the fellow man. Even in the centuries of the Renaissance and Reformation the Europeans were willing to believe the validity of traditional legends and superstitions, the existence of sorcerers and witches. Like other peoples and civilizations, they were concerned, above all, with man's fundamental and unchanging relationship to God and to the divine or demonic forces present in nature. Only in modern Western civilization a rational and critical element has entered these ancient relationships, and the emphasis has shifted more and more to interpersonal relationships, to the concern with fellow men, a development which gave rise to the growth of the social sciences in all their variety.

Thus the spirit of liberty, rationality and respect for the individual began, in the age of Enlightenment, to permeate all aspects of life and thought. It has created an unprecedented sense of legal security and thereby a climate that has favored the growth of economic enterprise and social initiative. Freedom has promoted well-being, and not the other way around as some people have recently assumed. It has freed the human mind for new discoveries and has accelerated the pace of development throughout. It has broken through ancient immobilities, and, by this emancipatory mobilization, become the greatest revolutionary force in the condition of man.

III

THE CONCEPT of a free man and of a free mind in an open society, which is the essence of modern civilization, represents a daring venture and a new phenomenon in history. Its acceptance marked one of these decisive transformations of all human life, which Karl Jaspers called axial times,[3] such an axial time was the sixth century B.C., when in Confucius and Lao-tzu, Buddha and

[3] See Karl Jaspers, Vom Ursprung und Ziel der Geschichte (Zürich: Artemis Verlag, 1949).

the Hebrew prophets, Greek philosophy and tragedy, man reached a new consciousness of himself and a deepened self-awareness. Such axial times originate in limited geographic areas but they have the tendency to become of universal historical significance. Modern civilization, too, rose in the geographically limited North Atlantic area but its influence has since spread all over the earth. By its inherent element of liberty, it presents the greatest difficulties in organizing society and in directing man. It, and it alone, has accepted all men as equal in principle and has recognized opposition as legitimate and as a constructive contribution both to the interplay of politics and to the growth of thought. It does not insist on uniformity; on the contrary, it regards a society as the more highly developed the more effectively it includes, on a basis of equality and freedom, various social classes, cultural traditions, religious faiths or ethnic groups and the more readily it welcomes a maximum variety of individual experiences.

In modern civilization the old ties with the help of which societies were held together and man was directed throughout the ages—Dostoevsky in his tale of the Grand Inquisitor identified these ties with the temptations held out by the Devil in the desert, miracle, mystery, and authority—do no longer enjoy their former dominant position. *Un roi, une loi, une foi* was as characteristic of the absolutism and the grandeur of the French monarchy under Louis XIV as Autocracy, Orthodoxy and Nationality was of Russia under Count Sergei Uvarov and Konstantin Pobedonostsev. Recently Communism, Fascism and some of the new nationalist states have revived this ancient basis of organized society and proclaimed it as something new and "progressive." But modern civilization rejects as the basis of its political and intellectual life unity of blood, of faith, of class and the belief in a community—racial, theocratic or ideological—as a vehicle of salvation.

With its human and all-too-human shortcomings, the United States represents in principle the most characteristic modern Western society. It came into being as the product of the seventeenth-century English revolutions and of the age of Enlightenment. In the eighteenth century Anglo-America presented to Europeans and Americans alike the reign of liberty and rationality contrasting with the despotism and superstition then still prevailing in Europe. Edward Gibbon in his "General Observations on the Fall of the Roman Empire in the West" mused about the possibility of new savage conquerors overrunning Europe and carrying slavery and desolation as far as the Atlantic Ocean. But this time "ten thousand vessels would transport beyond their [the conquerors'] pursuit the remains of civilized society; and Europe would revive and flourish in the American world, which is already filled with her colonies and institutions."

Even without a barbarian conquest the philosopher Bishop George Berkeley expressed in 1726 the feeling that Old Europe could not live up to the exalted hopes of the age and was decaying; he foresaw in Anglo-America the center of spiritual renovation, the rise of empire and of arts. Half a century later Abbé Raynal, then a very widely read author, drew a glowing picture of an America destined to bring about a new era of humanity, and set it up as an example for Europe. It seemed almost as if the air of America could change man because it was filled with liberty. This admiring appreciation of America was not confined to Britain and France. The old Goethe was deeply fascinated by the tolerance and liberty found in the United States and by its pioneering technological spirit. It is easily understandable that the Anglo-Americans shared this admiration. "If all the sovereigns of Europe were to set themselves to work, to emancipate the minds of their subjects from their present ignorance and prejudices," Thomas Jefferson wrote from Paris, then the center of European civilization, in 1787, "a thousand years would not place them on that high ground, on which our common people are now setting out." The keenest hopes and aspirations of the democratic revolution which swept Europe in the late eighteenth century seemed destined for realization in North America.[4]

Half a century later Alexis de Tocqueville saw in the United States the home and center of democracy. He was convinced that this democracy represented, at least for Western civilization, an irresistible and universal movement which aimed at the establishment of "l'égalité des conditions." This equality of conditions was to him the inescapable outcome of the transformation of the social body brought about through the democratic revolution

[4] See Hans Kohn, *The Idea of Nationalism*, op. cit., ch. VI, and *American Nationalism. An Interpretative Essay* (New York: Macmillan, 1957), ch. I.

which he believed irresistibly spreading over the globe. Tocqueville did not underrate the difficulties faced by democratic society, and that means by modern civilization. He had no easy illusions about the nature of man. "Men are in general neither too good nor too bad, they are mediocre," he wrote in a letter on January 3, 1843. "There are two men in every man; and if it is childish to see only one, it is completely sad and unjust to look only upon the other. . . . Man with his vices, his weaknesses, his virtues, his confused mixture of good and evil, of the low and the high, of honesty and depravity, still is on the whole the most worthy object of investigation, of interest, of compassion, of affection and of admiration, which can be found on earth. As we do not have angels, we cannot attach ourselves to anything which would be nobler and more worthy of our devotion than our fellow men."

Lord Acton in his "Lectures on the French Revolution" called Tocqueville the most widely acceptable of all the writers and the hardest to find fault with. At a time when political and social privileges still existed all over Europe and were accepted by most people as "natural" and indispensable, Tocqueville predicted the democratization, which could as well be called Americanization, of Europe. "Le gouvernement de la démocratie," he wrote, "fait descendre l'idée des droits politiques jusqu'au moindre des citoyens, comme la division des biens met l'idée du droit de propriété en général à la portée de tous les hommes. C'est là un de ses plus grands mérites à mes yeux. . . . It is impossible to understand how equality could fail to penetrate finally the political world as it does penetrate everything else. One cannot imagine men being for ever unequal among themselves in one point and equal in others. Thus they will finally arrive at a situation of full equality."

Tocqueville saw this as an inevitable process; he believed that the question was only whether this equality of modern civilization would arrive peacefully or by violence, whether it would increase liberty or establish despotism. The former happened in Britain and the United States, the latter in the major countries of the European continent. In the English-speaking homelands of the North Atlantic civilization the democratic principles are deeply rooted and are supported by the traditions of local self-government and decentralization. Such has not been the case in France or Italy, in Germany or Russia. There the forces of premodern society and the adoration of past grandeur and central authority have frequently challenged the conditions of modern civilization. This was of course much less the case in France than in Russia. But everywhere on the continent movements arose which openly and contemptuously rejected the principles of a free and open society which was born in the eighteenth century and which Tocqueville went to study in the United States.

Tocqueville clearly understood the difference between the North Atlantic countries and those on the European continent. "The English who emigrated three hundred years ago to found a democratic commonwealth on the shores of the New World had all learned to take a part in public affairs in their mother country," he wrote; "they were conversant with trial by jury; they were accustomed to liberty of speech and of the press, to personal freedom, to the notion of rights and the practice of asserting them. They carried with them to America these free institutions and manly customs, and these institutions preserved them against the encroachments of the state. Thus among the Americans as among the British it is freedom that is old; equality is of comparatively modern date. The reverse is occurring in continental Europe, where equality, introduced by absolute power under the rule of kings, was already infused into the habits of nations long before freedom entered into their thought."

Tocqueville was conscious of the threats which equality presents to free society. But his confidence in liberty as the supreme value was never shaken. He could have repeated what Montesquieu said in his "Dialogue de Sylla et d'Eucrate": "Les Dieux qui ont donné à la plupart des hommes une lâche ambition, ont attaché à la liberté presqu'autant de malheurs qu'à la servitude. Mais quel que doive être le prix de cette noble liberté, il faut bien le payer aux Dieux." With regard to liberty the lot of the Americans seemed singular to Tocqueville: "They have derived from the aristocracy of England the notion of private rights and the taste for local freedom; and they have been able to retain both because they have had no aristocracy to combat."

Tocqueville saw the "insane fear of socialism" as a threat to the liberties of modern civilization. It had thrown, as he wrote in 1852, the French middle class headlong into the arms of Napoleonic despotism. He despised those who welcomed an authoritarian government because they believed that it would strengthen religion and morality. The danger of such a welcome has been ever present in France and on the European continent, but today it is not unknown even in the United States, where some seem willing, in order to support "morality" and "religion," to enter into an alliance with, or support of, apparently religious authoritarian regimes similar to, or worse than, that established by Napoleon III. Tocqueville thought such attempts not only ethically but also practically unsound; he was convinced that the traditional society of inequality was doomed to disappear, "and that it only remains for the men of our times to organize progressively and prudently the new democratic society on its ruins." He firmly believed in the potential liberty and equality of all men. "My dominant feeling," he wrote expressing a sentiment significant in the first era of global history, "when I find myself in the presence of another human being no matter how humble his position, is that of the original equality of this species, and from then on I am concerned less perhaps to please or to serve him than not to offend his dignity."

Tocqueville thought and wrote as a liberal and at the same time as a Christian. In America he found the spirit of religion and the spirit of freedom, which were marching in France (as in other countries of continental Europe) in the opposite direction, intimately united. In his letters to Count Gobineau in January 1857 Tocqueville upheld the incompatibility of Christianity with doctrines of race. Is it not the unique trait of Christianity, he asked, "to have abolished those racial distinctions which the Jewish religion still retained and to have made therefrom but one human race, all of whose members are equally capable of improving and uniting themselves?" He rejected Gobineau's deep pessimism about modern civilization, a pessimism, anticipating the later fashionable anti-Western *Kulturpessimismus.* "You profoundly distrust mankind, at least our kind; you believe that it is not only decadent but incapable of ever lifting itself up again. . . . To me, human society, like persons, become something worthwhile only through their use of liberty. . . . No, I shall not believe that this human race . . . has become that bastardized flock of sheep which you say it is, and that nothing remains but to deliver it . . . to a small number of shepherds who, after all, are not better animals than are we, the human sheep, and who indeed are often worse."

In the last year of his life (1857), when political and religious reaction seemed triumphant on the European continent, Tocqueville expressed sentiments which are equally valid today: "I should have loved freedom, I believe, at all times, but in the time in which we live I am ready to worship it." Freedom to him was inseparable from the dignity of every individual and of all races, from the "égalité des conditions" which he saw as the goal of modern civilization. The concern with public welfare, with the amelioration of the condition of all men, found in the United States, he wished to introduce everywhere to make liberty more secure. He praised the French Revolution because it had equalized the tax burden, destroyed privileges which had favored the concentration of wealth in single hands, and had "infinitely" multiplied the chances which enabled men to move from poverty to a "comfortable position, even to being rich." This social mobility was first achieved in modern England and found its fruition in the United States.[5]

IV

TOCQUEVILLE shared with his friend John Stuart Mill the faith in the possible and necessary amelioration of the human condition, an optimistic faith which has characterized the outlook of the people of the United States. "Most of the great positive evils of the world are in themselves removable," Mill wrote in his *Utilitarianism*, "and will, if human affairs continue to improve, be in the end reduced within narrow limits. Poverty in any sense implying suffering may be completely extinguished by the wisdom of society combined with the good sense and providence of individuals. All the grand sources, in short, of human suffering are in a degree, many of them almost entirely, conquerable by human care and effort."

[5] See Edward T. Gargan, *Alexis de Tocqueville: The Critical Years 1848–1851* (Washington: Catholic University Press, 1955); Hans Barth, "Alexis de Tocqueville. Makelloser und Zwiespältiger Ruhm," *Neue Zürcher Zeitung*, 11 April 1959; John Lukacs (ed.), *Tocqueville: The European Revolution & Correspondence with Gobineau* (Doubleday Anchor Books, 1959).

But improvement in human conditions is not sufficient to assure the expansion of liberty. Mill thought that liberty and law were least threatened among Englishmen, perhaps because "in all questions between a government and an individual, the presumption in every Englishman's mind is that the government is in the wrong." Tolerance for fellow men and their opinions, distrust of power and its possible abuses, a dislike of violence, have rooted liberty more strongly in England than in other lands. But in the twentieth century the quest of liberty has spread far beyond the English isle, and has to be seen in its world-wide social frame. Mill stated the task before modern civilization in prophetic words: "How to unite the greatest individual liberty of action with the common ownership in the raw materials of the globe, and an equal participation of all in the benefits of combined labor."

The same concern for individual liberty and human welfare which characterized John Stuart Mill also characterized Lord Acton, A generation younger than Tocqueville and Mill, he shared with the former the aristocratic birth and the Catholic faith, with the latter, the dedication to individual liberty and to modern civilization. He, too, saw in the United States the most vigorous exponent of this civilization and the model of the future. His *Lectures on Modern History* which he delivered at the turn of the century at Cambridge University told the story, how in the course of the three centuries from the Renaissance and Reformation to the American Revolution, "by the combined efforts of the weak, made under compulsion, to resist the reign of force and constant wrong, liberty has been preserved, and secured, and extended, and finally understood." This process of the growth of tolerance, the rights of men, and the self-government of nations, which started in the Netherlands and in the Puritan Commonwealth, culminated in Anglo-America. Acton knew how closely connected liberty and welfare were. "There is no liberty where there is hunger," we read in one of his manuscript notes, "the theory of liberty demands strong efforts to help the poor. Not merely for safety, for humanity, for religion, but for liberty." Acton, a member of the upper class himself, opposed all forms of class government. "The danger is not that a particular class is unfit to govern," he wrote. "Every class is unfit to govern." And he insisted that "the poorer class . . . their interests are the most sacred."[6]

No historian expressed more clearly than Acton did the distrust of power which is one of the outstanding traits of modern Western civilization. In his "Inaugural Lecture on the Study of History" he warned to "suspect power more than vice." In his *Lectures on Modern History* he rejected the adoration of success and the social Darwinism so characteristic of the later nineteenth century. He took his stand with the powerless against the powerful. He valued a civilization which, against all vitalistic and utilitarian arguments, defended its weak against its strong. Progress of civilization has imposed increasing sacrifices on society, in behalf of those who can make no return, from whose welfare it derives no equivalent benefit. For civilization "depends on preserving, at infinite cost, which is infinite loss, the crippled child and the victim of accident, the idiot and the madman, the pauper and the culprit, the old and infirm, curable and incurable. This growing dominion of disinterested motive, this liberality towards the weak, in social life, corresponds to that respect for the minority, in political life, which is the essence of freedom." Acton distrusted great men more than little people. As a student of history he had no illusions about man or politics but he had the faith in human liberty and dignity which distinguishes modern civilization from all others. "History is not a web woven with innocent hands," he wrote in a manuscript note. "Among all the causes which degrade and demoralize men, power is the most constant and the most active."

The destruction of modern Western civilization in Russia in November, 1917 and in Germany in January, 1933 was facilitated by the climate of respect for authority prevailing in those countries. The Russian tradition of autocracy, of a dominant "Orthodox" ideology and of strong leadership from above was hardly changed but rather intensified by the shift from Czar to Commissar. From Hegel and Ranke on, Germany's historians endowed the demoniac temptations of power with the halo of a philosophy which they extolled for its "deep" understanding of the forces of

[6] See Lord Acton, *Lectures on Modern History* (New York: Schocken Paperbacks, 1961) and Gertrude Himmelfarb, *Lord Acton. A Study in Conscience and Politics* (University of Chicago Press, 1952).

history and nature. They admired the "immanent power-drive and vitality of great states"; the conflicts of interest and ensuing wars among nations appeared to them inevitable as the laws of nature. "In the [modern] Western concept man sins by the abuse of power," a contemporary German historian wrote in 1951; "in [the German and Russian] concept man sins by revolting against power." Perhaps it might be more just to replace the word "power" by "authority."

The distrust of power which Acton voiced forms a perennial criterion in the evaluation of government. In recent times, the growth of industrial technology and the vastness and complexity of organization have made the task of preserving liberty against the preponderance of bureaucracy in government, business and labor more difficult and more urgent. The danger involved for democracy in the "managerial revolutions" or in new power elites may, however, be overestimated, if the environment in which they develop is not sufficiently taken into account. Similarities of an outward nature are then easily overstressed and the fundamental difference between the core lands of modern Western civilization and the lands of the new industrial-bureaucratic despotisms are neglected. Under the guise of obeying the trend of history or of assuring the welfare of the people these new despotisms tend to reject the foundations of modern civilization, the right to opposition and to criticism, the sense for moderation and fair play.

Where liberty is deeply rooted, it has a power of reasserting itself against all glorification of authority. It is not without significance that Dwight D. Eisenhower—by his upbringing and achievements one of the outstanding military men of the West—has restated in his farewell address as President of the United States on January 17, 1961, Acton's distrust of power. "This conjunction of an immense military establishment and large arms industry is new in American experience," he said. "The total influence—economic, political, even spiritual—is felt in every city, every state house, every office of the federal government. We recognize the imperative need for this development. Yet we must not fail to comprehend its grave implications. Our toil, resources and livelihood are all involved; so is the very structure of our society. In the councils of government, we must guard against the acquisition of unwarranted influence, whether sought or unsought, by the military-industrial complex. The potential for the disastrous rise of misplaced power exists and will persist. We must never let the weight of this combination endanger our liberties or democratic processes. We should take nothing for granted. Only an alert and knowledgeable citizenry can compel the proper meshing of the huge industrial and military machinery of defense with our peaceful methods and goals so that security and liberty may prosper together. . . .

"In holding scientific research and discovery in respect, as we should, we must also be alert to the equal and opposite danger that public policy could itself become the captive of a scientific-technological elite. It is the task of statesmanship to mold, to balance, and to integrate these and other forces, new and old, within the principles of our democratic system—ever aiming toward the supreme goals of our free society. . . . Down the long lane of the history yet to be written America knows that this world of ours, ever-growing smaller, must avoid becoming a community of dreadful fear and hate, and be, instead, a proud confederation of mutual trust and respect. Such a confederation must be one of equals. The weakest must come to the conference table with the same confidence as do we, protected as we are by our moral, economic and military strength. That table, though scarred by many past frustrations, cannot be abandoned for the certain agony of the battlefield." Thus at a critical time for modern Western civilization, its principles of a fundamentally universal, civilian, libertarian and egalitarian society were restated.

V

MODERN civilization with its reliance on the individual and his self-determination, with its never-resting search for truth and promotion of welfare, burdens man inevitably with disturbing feelings of insecurity and loneliness. Then he searches for the security of the closed community and conformity as they existed in premodern civilizations, or he overemphasizes the uniqueness and superiority of the strong individual who dares to stand alone.

Conformity is inherent in all primitive societies, where the group counts for more than the individual, who without questioning accepts its authority, values and standards. Pre-modern civilizations regard the heretic as the archenemy, the embodiment of evil. The man who thinks differently presents the dogmatic, closed or absolutist society with a challenge which it cannot accept and which it answers by violence or coercive means. Only in modern times has the right of the individual to think for himself been recognized. The essential calling and duty of man, as Emerson saw it, was to conduct his own life and not to have it manufactured for him; a right nation would be a nation consisting of such independent individuals and nonconformists. It was Emerson's hope that the United States would be such a nation. He deeply distrusted power, wealth, bigness of all kinds, which would threaten the independence of the individual. "The truest test of civilization," he wrote, "is not the census, not the size of cities, nor crops—but the kind of man the country turns out. When I look over this constellation of cities which animate and illustrate the land, and see how little the government has to do with their daily life, how self-helped and self-directed all families are . . . man acting on man by weight of opinion, of longer or better directed industry; the refining influence of women; the invitation which experience and permanent causes open to youth and labor; when I see how much each virtuous and gifted person, whom all men consider, lives affectionately with scores of excellent people who are not known far from home, and perhaps with great reason, reckons these people his superiors in virtue and in symmetry and force of their qualities—I see what cubic values America has, and in these a better certificate of civilization than great cities or enormous wealth."

At the same time Emerson was painfully aware of the fact that American life did not live up to his idea of it. "Out of doors all seems a market; indoors, an airtight stove of conventionalism," he complained in his address "The Young American" in 1844. "They recommend conventional virtues, whatever will earn and preserve property . . . whatever goes to secure, adorn, enlarge these is good; whatever jeopardizes any of these is damnable." The opposition was no better. "They attack the great capitalists, but with the aim to make a capitalist of the poor man. The opposition is against those who have money from those who wish to have money. But who announces to us in journal, or in pulpit, or in street, the secret of heroism? . . . The more need of a withdrawal from the crowd, and a resort to the fountain of right, by the brave. The timidity of our public opinion is our disease, or, shall I say, the publicness of opinion, the absence of private opinion." The heroism which Emerson meant did not mean national self-assertion but the strength of the independent individual to stand up against the opinions and prejudices of the group. "Nationality is often silly," Emerson wrote in his *Journal*. "Every nation believes that the Divine Providence has a sneaking kindness for it." The American spirit appealed to Emerson "not because it was American but because it was a self-reliant faith in the present and the future."

Yet individual self-reliance can lead to self-assertive arrogance which claims for the individual or the group higher rights than those of the common man. Oswald Spengler saw in Faust the typical representative of modern Western civilization. Faust's titanism is one of the dangers inherent in Western civilization; it is as little of its essence as conformity is. Faust is more a Renaissance than a modern man. He belongs to the moral climate of an era in which artists began to assert their privileges and separateness as exceptional men. "An awful habit has developed among common people and even among the educated to whom it seems natural that painters of highest distinction must show signs of some ghastly and nefarious vice alike with the capricious and eccentric temperament," Giovan Battista Armenini wrote in his *Dei veri precetti della pittura* (1586). "And the worst is that many ignorant artists believe to be very exceptional by affecting melancholy and eccentricity."

In the proud feeling of his freedom modern man in his thirst for knowledge, for creative expansion, for the fullness of life tends to step out of the bounds of common humanity. To the young Goethe—he was then twenty-four years old—Prometheus appeared as the representative of an extreme individualism, the model of the proud artist who God-like in his creative force has no need of God or fellow men.

> Didst thou not accomplish all thyself,
> Holy glowing heart?

In this interpretation Prometheus is the model of the arrogance and presumption of the man of genius, the individual who owes everything to himself, to his daring and strength—be he Napoleon or a creator-artist—and who thereby surges high above the common human lot.

An older brother of the modern superman was Christopher Marlowe's *Doctor Faustus*. His end was tragic, a triumph of religion over magic, of hell over man. The greatest writer of modern times, Goethe, looked upon Faust with different eyes. His Faust, too, was an overreacher who demanded not only knowledge and dominion but the intensification of life and of all human experience.

> And all of life for all mankind created
> Shall be within mine inmost being tested:
> The highest, lowest forms my soul shall borrow,
> Shall heap upon itself their bliss and sorrow,
> And thus, my own soul self to all their selves expanded,
> I too, at last, shall with them all be stranded.

Voluntaristic impatience and arrogance, an ever-present danger in modern man, inspires the scene in the study when Faust, himself a scholar and intellectual, rejects the Word in favor of the Deed. In his pessimistic titanism Faust refuses to accept life as it is. He curses hope and above all patience; and as a consequence is accused by the spirits of having destroyed the beautiful world.

> Fluch sei der Hoffnung! Fluch dem Glauben,
> Und Fluch vor allem der Geduld!

When Mephistopheles warns him that the all and whole, that the absolute is not for man, Faust replies, "Allein ich will!" (Ah, but I will!). In his titanic restlessness, Faust is the representative of the modern homeless man who is lured by the abyss, Baudelaire's *gouffre*, and who is willing to take the suicidal risk:

> Bin ich der Flüchtling nicht? der Unbehauste?
> Der Unmensch ohne Zweck und Ruh,
> Der wie ein Wassersturz von Fels zu Felsen brauste,
> Begierig wütend, nach dem Abgrund zu?

I am the fugitive, all homeless roaming,
The monster without goal or rest,
Who like a cataract, down rocks and gorges foaming,
Leaps, maddened, into the abyss's breast.

But this Faust, the archetypal man of Goethe's youthful passion and of the Storm and Stress periods of modern civilization, is neither representative of Goethe nor of modern civilization. Their greatness is the ability to outgrow and overcome the Faustian temptation. The mature Goethe knew about the limitations of man and yet trusted man's nature and his greatness.

> *Nur allein der Mensch*
> *Vermag das Unmögliche:*
> *Er unterscheidet,*
> *Wählet und richtet;*
> *Er kann dem Augenblick*
> *Dauer verleihen.*
> *Er allein darf . . .*
> *Heilen und retten,*
> *Alles Irrende, Schweifende*
> *Nützlich verbinden.*

(Man alone can do the impossible. He distinguishes, chooses and judges. He can give to the moment lasting endurance. He alone can . . . heal and rescue, usefully join all that is erring and straying.)

In another poem, "Dedication," with which he opened the first edition of his collected works, the lady of his heart who after his youthful aberration was the source of his moral strength and mental recovery addressed him saying:

> *Kaum bist du Herr vom ersten Kinderwillen,*
> *So glaubst du dich schon Uebermensch genug,*
> *Versäumst die Pflicht des Mannes zu erfüllen!*
> *Wie viel bist du von andern unterschieden?*
> *Erkenne dich, leb mit der Welt in Frieden!*

(No sooner you feel yourself master of your juvenile will than you think that you are a singular human being, a superman, and neglect to fulfill the duty of a man. Know yourself and live at peace with the world!)

This poem expressed Goethe's concept of the mission of a poet, which like that of all other men, is to advance humanity and humanization, and that means for the individual, free self-determination through self-mastery, and for society, helpful co-operation. It is the poet's task to communicate through poetry to his "brothers" the path to the truth of life. By so doing, poetry relieves mankind from the heavy burden of life: "Day becomes lovely, night becomes bright."

Goethe's mature humanism followed this youthful titanism as Mozart's *Magic Flute* followed *Don Giovanni*. Faust and Don Giovanni are Renaissance figures; the message of Goethe's humanism, of the *Magic Flute*, of Beethoven's *Ninth Symphony*, of Lessing's *Nathan the Wise*, and of Kant's ethical universalism, are of the eighteenth century, of the very substance of modern civilization. This message is fundamentally hopeful of man and mankind, yet its optimism is tempered by the consciousness of the complexity and aberrations of all human life and striving. "Never, perhaps, have individuals isolated themselves and separated from one another more than at present," Goethe wrote. "Each one would like to personate the universe and to represent it from within himself." But he knew "that only mankind as a whole is truly man and that the individual can only be joyful and happy if he has the courage to feel himself part of the whole"— the whole being mankind and not any national or parochial group. Goethe was convinced that every individual potentiality is important and must be developed. "Only all men constitute humanity, only all forces taken together constitute the world." Goethe's faith in the universal validity of humanity found its most beautiful expression in his *Iphigenie*.

The same message of humanism and hope opens and concludes the second part of the Faust tragedy. Faithful to his optimistic humanism, Goethe did not finish his *Faust* as a tragedy. The play did not end with damnation and hell as did its Renaissance archetype. In the opening scene of the second part Faust, awakening from the shattering Gretchen tragedy, greets the mild dawn of morning, and gratefully praises the constancy of the earth which wraps him round with gladness. Glorifying life and nature, he utters no cry of anguish and does not indulge in personal complaint or self-pity. And when later on, in one of the marvelous poetic evocations of the glory of youth, his and Helena's son Euphorion rejoices in the tempestuousness and daring of the Storm and Stress, his father warns him against audacity and extreme passion, against "das Verwegne und überlebendige, heftige Triebe," and extols instead gentleness and moderation. Though Euphorion's playful artistry surpasses in beauty and grace by far that of the Faust of the first part, the Faust of the second part rejects this spectacle of Dionysian exuberance and strength and prays for its end. Euphorion's call for dangerous living, for war and victory, elicits from the chorus the sober reply that who in peace ever wishes the coming of war has severed himself from hope and happiness—key words of modern civilization.

The mature Goethe remained mindful of the common man and trustful of the power of humane moderation. He knew that excessive enthusiasm and excessive pessimism equally endanger the delicate fabric of modern civilization. The second part of *Faust* is pervaded throughout by Goethe's deep distrust—in which he was at one with men like Mill or Acton—of state-power and of the superman. Goethe's *Faust* is a refutation of Spengler's pessimistic identification of an overreaching Faust as the true representative of modern civilization. Spengler's Faust is a Renaissance superman or a German romanticist unmindful of the limits which common sense and common humanity have set to make possible a tolerable existence in the complex and pluralistic world of modern times. "There is nothing sadder to behold," Goethe warned, "than the sudden striving for the unconditional in this thoroughly conditioned world; in the year 1830 it seems perhaps more improper than ever."

Like Kant, Goethe had learned to respect human nature and the work of every individual. As a great poet and reader of the human heart he knew that individual and collective passions and overreaching aspirations are ever-present to threaten and confuse civilization. He regarded them as a heritage and survival of a primitive past and often of tribal and heroic idolatry. But he did not think that this impact of the past was inescapable. "I do not like the expression of raging passions," he wrote in 1807. "For

wherever a tiny human spark glints, I am happy to approve."
Throughout his mature life Goethe upheld the cosmopolitan
freedom of the mind, the wisdom of moderation and tolerance—
the fundamental values of modern civilization.[7]

VI

NO CIVILIZATION has consistently lived up to its values; none
has been as novel, complex and difficult as modern civilization and
therefore as much threatened by ever-renewed doubts, denials
and self-abandonment, by ever-repeated reassertion of the tribal
and national past, of historical myth and superstitions. In all
civilizations above the primitive level eccentrics and outsiders were
to be found, but until recently man felt securely embedded in the
strict framework of caste and tribe, of religion and rite, faithfully
observing the conventions and obeying the taboos of his particular
society. Conformism was the normal and universally accepted
attitude; it did not present a problem. In the Western world in
the nineteenth and twentieth centuries there has been less conformism than anywhere before. But since modern civilization
began to emancipate the individual and to demand his self-determination and independence from custom and authority—and the
first sonorous voice heard to that purpose was Milton's—conformism has become a problem. Emerson and Mill, Ibsen and
Nietzsche, have called upon modern man to beware of its danger.
The lonely pioneer or frontiersman who abandoned the security
of group and tradition and dared to challenge conventions and
taboos has been accepted as a representative figure of modern
civilization.

The same emancipation from social convention and traditional
restriction which made conformism a problem and in the last
years an object of lament for many writers and prophets of doom,
facilitated also the rise of men and movements which arrogated
to themselves special rights and asserted their superiority or privileges allegedly bestowed upon them by God, nature or history.

[7] See Karl Viëtor, Goethe, the Poet (Harvard University Press, 1949);
E. M. Butler, The Fortunes of Faust (Cambridge University Press, 1952);
Hans Kohn, The Mind of Germany (New York: Charles Scribner's Sons,
1960), ch. II.

Again, such attitudes were "normal" before the rise of modern civilization. The Chosen People and Promised Land ideas are of very ancient origin and have been hallowed by religious sanction. So have the privileges of families and classes claiming Divine grace as the justification for their unique position high above the common man or above other classes. The new opportunities provided by the great age of emancipation which started with the Enlightenment offered previously unprivileged men and groups the chance of emulating the former "divinely" chosen superior classes, races and supermen. This opportunity could be, like every opportunity, abused. Alexander and Caesar came of ancient aristocratic stock; the new phenomenon in Buonaparte was not that he claimed domination and that he stretched out his hands for world imperial goals, but that he came from the lower strata of society, a man from nowhere, who rose almost to the stars by his own daring, self-confidence and power, unaided by tradition or ancestral privilege. In a similar way, Karl Marx raised a whole class from the depth of society where they were lost in the anonymity of procreating hewers of wood and drawers of water into the predestined masters and saviors of mankind. The rise of new supermen and super-groups was made possible by the mobility of modern civilization. But at the same time its critical and rational mood and its egalitarian concern for all men, irrespective of ancestry or occupation, tended toward a more objective view of the rights of individuals and peoples, divesting them from religious or pseudoreligious sanction for their privileges.

By its social mobility and its technological transformation of distances into neighborhoods, modern civilization has increased tensions and widened the possibilities of conflict. It encourages striving for excelling or surpassing qualities and achievements. A strong competitive element is inherent in the unceasing quest, in the ever-unsettling progress of modern life. But these trends are tempered by considerations for general welfare, for equal rights, for the maximation of happiness and hopefulness, as far as they depend on social measures and the public will. Though these considerations are often sinned against by individuals, by corporate groups and above all by races and nations, they tend ultimately to assert themselves, wherever modern civilization, a very young and experimental civilization, has struck roots. In spite of its dynamism, it understands the creative strength of long-range moderation and patience. Among peoples where modern civilization has not firmly taken root, decisive action and "red-blooded vitality" have recently been extolled as against "anemic" indecision and "sentimental" humanitarianism of which modern civilization has often been accused. In times of unprecedented changes—compared with other civilizations modern civilization presents permanent and ever-accelerated change—it is as dangerous to expect too much as it is to demand too little. Man can never solve all problems but he must always try to solve, though imperfectly, as many of them as possible. Fatalism is as alien to modern civilization as is messianism or utopianism. Absolute justice or total liberty cannot be established on this earth, but free men can always and everywhere combat injustice or oppression and must do it above all in their own community. They can loosen some chains, alleviate some burdens and gladden some hearts. Modern civilization does not carry a message of salvation but one of hope, for this and future generations, on this earth and throughout its entire expanse.

VII

THE EMPHASIS on future and hope characterizes Western civilization. Future in the sense used here has nothing in common with the futurism of Marinetti or Mayakovsky, an early twentieth-century artistic movement which represented an anti-Western caricature of the modern age. It started in pre-Fascist Italy and had a brief flowering at the birth time of Russian bolshevism. It was one of the distress signs of countries which suffered from the sudden onrush of modern industrialism into a still premodern society.

The emphasis on future and hope was strongest in the United States. Walt Whitman was its foremost poet. Tocqueville in his concluding remarks in Democracy in America wrote about the emerging modern society: "Although the revolution which is taking place in the social condition, the laws, the opinions, and the feelings of men is still very far from being terminated, yet its results already admit of no comparison with anything that the world has ever before witnessed. I go back from age to age up to the remotest antiquity, but I find no parallel to what is occurring before my eyes. . . ."

No previous civilization has been similarly directed toward the future and animated by the knowledge that man can and will by his effort change many of the ills and evils under which he had patiently suffered throughout the ages. Understandably this expectation has often degenerated into a dogma of rapid and inevitable progress which within a foreseeable future might produce ideal conditions on earth. Chiliastic utopianism, so well-known from premodern civilizations and religious movements, presents a danger to modern civilization, too. But as this civilization ran into difficulties caused by the nature of man and things and by the perseverance of traditional attitudes and myths, the opposite danger, also well-known from the past, began to menace modern civilization. People turned from the self-confidence and over-optimism of the nineteenth century to the pessimistic vision of an apocalyptic age, in which modern civilization and its freedom would perish.

Such laments are as old as are those over the corruption and vice of the age, over the inroads of technology and materialism, over war and barbarism. Technical progress and its accompanying curse worried Horace in the Augustan age (Odes I, 3):

> Daring all their goal to win,
> Men tread forbidden ground and rush on sin. . . .
> Nought is there for man too high;
> Our impious folly e'en would climb the sky. . . .

The horror of war made Horace foresee (Epode 16) a Rome ruined:

> Amid her streets, her temples nigh,
> The mountain wolf shall unmolested lie.
> O'er her cold ashes the barbarians ride. . . .

and he called upon the Romans to flee to the blessed islands of the west and to swear to return no more. Similarly in the religious wars of the sixteenth century Étienne de la Boétie lamented in a poem to his friend Montaigne: "What fate decreed for us to be born in times like these! My country perishes before my eyes and I see no other way but to emigrate, to leave my house, and to go wherever fate carries me. . . . When at the threshold of our century a new world rose out of the ocean, it happened because the gods wished to create a refuge where men under a better sky can cultivate their fields, while the cruel sword and ignominious plague condemn Europe to perish."

The feeling of appalling insecurity and the dread of unspeakable horrors have haunted mankind many times. But formerly cruelty and oppression were accepted as a matter of course; modern civilization has heightened our moral sensibility so that we protest, and recoil from, behavior and relationships which former generations and other civilizations accepted as "natural." The revolution of rising expectations which started in Anglo-America in the eighteenth century and is today sweeping the globe, means more than economic and technological advancement. It is distinguished by new and higher demands upon public morality and civic responsibility and by hope for a greater dignity of human life. It was this revolution of rising expectations which established the superiority of the modern West over other civilizations. Today this superiority tends to diminish and to disappear because the revolution has become global.

Until recent times the West was in no way superior to other civilizations. In refinement of living and in cultural achievements, the Levant, at the time of the Crusades, far excelled the Occident. One of the causes of the Crusades was the overpopulation and famine in backward and, compared with the East, barbarian Europe of the period. Islamic and Arab culture influenced the intellectual growth of the West. In eleventh-century Spain a large number of Arabic works was translated into Latin and many Europeans "came to drink at the well of Moslem learning." The most brilliant member of the Hohenstaufen dynasty, Emperor Frederick II, in the first half of the thirteenth century, admired Arab civilization for the breadth of its views and the greater freedom of its intellectual atmosphere. Half a century later the greatest of Christian medieval travelers, Marco Polo, reported the wonders of the large cities which he found in Asia. Only in the seventeenth century did the West establish its superiority based upon its consciousness of breaking through ancient traditions and upon its venturesome spirit. By the middle of the nineteenth century the West was convinced of the permanence of its temporary superiority. Ranke wrote in 1879 that "the spirit of the West subdues the world." This very success, however, marked the beginning of the end of Western superiority.

VIII

THE BLINDNESS of modern civilization to the change in relationship involved in the course of history is the more astonishing when we recall that Western civilization was the first to understand the historical nature of man and of all his thought and activities. There has been in the past great historical writing before the rise of modern civilization, especially among the Greeks. There have been peoples like the Jews and the Chinese who were deeply conscious of their past and its impact on the present. There has been an insistence upon impartiality and objectivity of historiography which goes as far as a present-day scientist could ever demand. Lucian, a Greek sceptic who lived in the second century of our era, gave the following description of the ideal historian: "Fearless, incorruptible, free, a friend of free expression and the truth, intent . . . on calling a fig a fig and a trough and trough, giving nothing to hatred or to friendship, sparing no one, showing neither pity nor shame nor obsequiousness, an impartial judge, well disposed to all men up to the point of not giving one side more than its due, in his books a stranger and a man without a country, independent, subject to no sovereign, not reckoning what this or that man will think, but stating the facts."[8] And Pierre Bayle of Rotterdam wrote at the beginning of the eighteenth century that "a historian as historian is like Melkhisedekh, without father, without mother and without ancestors. Asked whence he comes, he must reply: I am neither French nor German, neither English nor Spanish: I am a citizen of the world. I serve neither emperor nor the King of France, but truth alone: she is my only queen to whom I swore obedience."

The Enlightenment has sometimes been regarded as an age of reason without an understanding for history. But it was not by accident that modern civilization, which has its roots in the

[8] Lucian's essay, "How to Write History," in Loeb Classical Library, Lucian, vol. VI.

Enlightenment, has become the most history-conscious civilization: the curiosity of the Enlightenment and its critical sense extended to history, too. Only since the eighteenth century has history prospered as a science with its research in the sources and its critical analysis of all traditions. Historical science has since opened up entirely new vistas, not inferior therein to the natural sciences. It has uncovered distant and unknown pasts, applied new methods, brought anthropology, psychology and the social sciences to bear upon our understanding of our own past and to the exploration of all other civilizations. It has restored to the non-Western peoples the consciousness of their own history and has drawn them into the growing realization of the unity of history and mankind. Thus modern civilization was at one and the same time the most revolutionary civilization pushing toward ever-new frontiers and the most history-conscious one. As it had discovered the space dimension of the globe, so it widened the time dimension of history. These achievements carried with them dangerous implications for Western civilization. The dynamism of its innovating spirit made it vulnerable to utopian expectations and to overweening pride; its historism made it vulnerable to the tyranny of the past. The fascination of the past was perhaps least dangerous in the United States, a nation born in the Enlightenment and which Goethe in a well-known poem in 1827 praised for being more fortunate than Europe for having no ruined castles, no venerable stones, no useless memories and no feuds of the past, to prevent the Americans from living in the present.

In other nations modern nationalism enhanced the fascination of the past over the living generations. The nation, the product of a long history, has been seen as the creator of all cultural values. "All great things," Ernst Moritz Arndt wrote at the beginning of the nineteenth century, "which a man does, forms, thinks, and invents as a hero, an artist, a law giver, or an inventor—all that comes to him only from the nation." The nation, it was believed, determines man, his thought and feelings and this nation was assumed to go back with its substance unchanged for two thousand years and more. Arndt, like so many German nationalists, appealed to Tacitus, the Roman writer, as a witness for the continuity of the German character. Tacitus, Arndt proudly remarked, prophesied the splendid future of the Germans on account of their moral and racial purity. "But of all things, he realized," Arndt wrote, "how important it was for their future greatness and majesty that they preserved the purity of their blood and resembled only themselves," that they were leading a truly German life in the full sense of the word without alien influences. Similarly Mazzini and Mussolini appealed to the greatness of Rome of two thousand years ago as the guide post for modern Italians. The fascination of history supported a self-centered nationalism and rejected the cosmopolitan liberalism which had accompanied the rise of modern Western civilization. Among the historical forces in the early part of the twentieth century, nationalism was foremost in weakening Western civilization to a degree that it doubted its own foundations of individual liberty and of free cosmopolitan intercourse.

IX

NATIONALISM sparked the European war in 1914. The unresolved nationalist aspirations and conflicts which had plagued central Europe since 1848 set the fire ablaze. It did not remain confined to central Europe. It spread as a result of the German attempt to establish their European hegemony for which they had laid the foundation under Bismarck. This challenge to the European balance of power aroused Britain's opposition.[9] Soon the war degenerated into an ideological civil war within Western civilization. Russia and Germany, though in ways varying according to their own traditions, seceded from, and turned against, Western civilization. After having won the war, the Western democracies refused to take the needed bold historical initiative in building a new order to revitalize the civilization for which they claimed to stand. They did not realize the deep wounds which the war and its consequences had inflicted upon the European mind nor the transformation in power relationship on a global scale which the war had brought about.

Paul Valéry expressed in "La crise de l'esprit" (1919) his fear that as a result of the war Europe would lose her global leadership

[9] See Ludwig Dehio, *Germany and World Politics in the Twentieth Century* (New York: Knopf, 1959), a collection of five essays which offer the best introduction to an understanding of the origins and nature of the two World Wars of the twentieth century.

and become what she really was, a little cape of the Asian continent. Looking back on the war, he commented in a lecture "L'Européen" (1922) on the general restlessness and uncertainty which characterized the immediate postwar years, as if the storm which had died away were about to break. "There is no thinking man, however shrewd or learned he may be, who can hope to dominate this anxiety, to escape from this impression of darkness, to measure the probable duration of this period, when the vital relations of humanity are profoundly disturbed. One can say that all the fundamentals of our world have been affected by the war, or more exactly, by the circumstances of the war; something deeper has been worn away than the renewable parts of the machine. You know how greatly the general economic situation has been disturbed, and the polity of states, and the very life of the individual. . . . But among all these endured things is the Mind. The Mind has indeed been cruelly wounded . . . it passes a mournful judgment on itself. It doubts itself profoundly."

The war of 1914 with its unexpectedly long duration, its hecatombs and distress in the trenches, its frenzy of hedonism and profiteering in the hinterland, undermined and destroyed the confidence in the validity of Western civilization. The crisis had set in before, in the visions and predictions of nineteenth-century artists and intellectuals, whose wish-projections became an actuality with a vengeance in the twentieth century. In the decade before the war the crisis gained momentum, with the growing impact of the apocalyptic and feverish mood of Dostoevsky on the West, with German expressionism, with the new trends in the visual arts and in music. But it was only the war—and in the United States the depression a decade later—which revealed the depth of the crisis of modern civilization. Seemingly triumphant in the war, democracy or Western civilization emerged in reality weakened. The rise and advance of Fascism and Communism were not due to their intrinsic value or to the shortcomings of the peace treaty—after all Russia, Italy, Japan were not among the nations victimized at Versailles—but to the lack of creative vigor and courageous vision in the leading Western nations, the United States and Great Britain. The stagnation was not caused by economic factors, for the United States, at least, was in the 1920's advertised, to its own citizens and to the dazzled Europeans, as a miracle of prosperity. The roots of the stagnation lay in spiritual fatigue, in apparent exhaustion of the inspirational springs of Western civilization, which expressed itself in cynicism and in a strange mixture of despair and complacency. Personal egotism was matched by national egotism which led to a policy of isolationism and of mutual recriminations among the Western nations.

Indicative of the crisis was the corruption of pacifism, which— legitimate as a moral pattern of life, as a witness to sacrifice and martyrdom, and as such a salt of the earth and a reminder of verities—began to cater to the egotism and hedonism of the people, promising them peace and happiness if only they would not fight for their fellow men. By a supreme irony the pacifists in the 1930's helped the most antipacific force on earth. From there it was only a slight step to a pacifism asserting that Fascism really meant peace, in a more or less veiled way accepting many of its pretexts and accusations, and finally justifying the aggressors and finding faults with their victims. The principle of nonresistance to evil degenerated into a denial that evil exists, into an appeal to accept the evil and to condone injustice. Thus pacifism, which is a reminder and a witness of the verities, became in the twenties and thirties one of the elements which could be used and abused by Fascism for the destruction of the verities.

A few thinkers understood in 1917—the decisive year of the period—that modern civilization and its liberties could survive after the war only by outgrowing self-centered nationalism and imperialism. Norman Angell wrote then in his book *The Political Conditions of Allied Success:* "The survival of the Western democracies, in so far as that is a matter of the effective use of their force, depends upon their capacity to use it as a unit, during the war and after. That unity we have not attained, even for the purposes of the war, because we have refused to recognize its necessary conditions—a kind and degree of democratic internationalism to which current political ideas and feelings are hostile; an internationalism which is not necessary to the enemy, but is to us. He can in some measure ignore it. We cannot. His unity, in so far as it rests upon moral factors, can be based upon the old nationalist conceptions; our unity depends upon a revision of them, an enlargement into an internationalism. The greatest obstacle to a permanent association of nations by which the security of each shall be made to rest upon the strength of the whole are disbelief in its feasibility and our subjection to the traditions of national sovereignty and independence. Were it generally believed in, and desired, it would be not only feasible but inevitable. Return to the old relationships after the war will sooner or later doom the democratic nations, however powerful each may be individually, to subjugation in detail by a group, inferior in power but superior in material unity—a unity which autocracy achieves at the cost of freedom and human worth." This analysis of 1917 was borne out by the events in 1940.

A similar understanding of the forces determining the course of Germany and Japan in World War I was shown by Thorstein Veblen, who wrote in January, 1917 *An Enquiry into the Nature of Peace and Terms of Its Perpetuation*, a work indebted to Immanuel Kant. "Chief among the relevant circumstances in the current situation," he wrote, "are the imperial designs of Germany and Japan. These two national establishments are very much alike . . . both in effect are incorrigibly bent on warlike enterprise. And in neither case will considerations of equity, humanity, decency, veracity, or the common good be allowed to trouble the quest of dominion." Veblen faced the question of how a peace compact could be established with these two powers, which, on account of their semi-feudal character, he called "dynastic" states. Anticipating in 1917 the course of events in the following three decades, Veblen warned that any peace compact with Germany and Japan "will necessarily be equivalent to arranging a period of recuperation for a new onset of dynastic enterprise. . . . Consummation of imperial mastery being the highest . . . end of all endeavor, its pursuit not only relieves its votaries from the observance of any minor obligations that run counter to its needs, but it also imposes a moral obligation to make the most of any opportunity for profitable deceit and chicanery that may offer. In short, the dynastic statesman is under the governance of a higher morality, binding him to the service of his nation's ambition to which it is his dutiful privilege loyally to devote all his powers of force and fraud. Democratically-minded persons may have some difficulty in appreciating the moral austerity of this spirit of devotion, and in seeing how its paramount exigence will set aside all meticulous scruples of personal rectitude and veracity, as being a shabby withholding of service due. This attitude of loyalty may perhaps be made intelligible by calling to mind the analogous self-surrender of the religious devotee."

Veblen was one of the few who in 1916 demanded that the United States enter the war in its own self-interest. "America is placed in an extra-hazardous position," he wrote, "between the two seas beyond which to either side lie the two Imperial Powers whose place in the modern economy of nations it is to disturb the peace in an insatiable quest of dominion. This position is no longer defensible in isolation, under the later state of the industrial arts, and the policy of isolation that has guided the national policy hitherto is therefore falling out of date. . . . Intervening seas can no longer be counted on as a decisive obstacle. On this latter head, what was reasonably true fifteen years ago is doubtful today, and it is in all reasonable expectation invalid for the situation fifteen years hence. The other peoples that are of a neutral temper may need the help of America sorely enough in their endeavors to keep the peace, but America's need of cooperation is sorer still, for the Republic is coming into a more precarious place than any of the others."

Veblen's words were as little heeded as those of Norman Angell. True, the peace treaties of 1919 introduced in the establishment of the League of Nations and of the International Labor Office (Part I and Part XIII of the Treaty of Versailles) the most promising and daring forward steps in international relations. The League of Nations was intended to become the instrument of a "universal dominion of right by such a concert of free peoples as shall bring peace and safety to all nations and make the world itself at last free." The concern for social justice and for the well-being, physical, moral and intellectual, of industrial wage-earners everywhere was declared of supreme international importance. But these good intentions were not taken seriously. Western civilization denied itself. Nationalism, imperialism, social inequalities not only continued but were exacerbated by growing nationalist and class antagonism, especially among the newly established nations in central-eastern Europe. The United States, Britain and France hardly set a better example. "If America should not take the leading part in this new enterprise of concerted power," Woodrow Wilson warned in 1919, "the world would experience one of those reversals of sentiment, one of those penetrating chills of reaction, which would lead to a universal cynicism. . . ." This happened. The "lost generation" feeling became characteristic of the 1920's throughout the Western world and helped the anti-Western movements to achieve their successes by promising to fill a vacuum. A period of "debunking" set in, modern civilization was "unmasked" as a hollow pretext for national egotism and economic interests.

The disintegration of Western civilization and of peace went hand in hand. Their interdependence was clearly foreseen by Woodrow Wilson. "Germany would not have gone into this war if she had thought Great Britain was going into it, and she most certainly would never have gone into this war if she dreamt America was going into it," he said in Columbus, Ohio, in September, 1919. "Unless there is this assurance of combined action before wrong is attempted, wrong will be attempted just as soon as the most ambitious nation can recover from the financial stress of this war." If America fulfilled Germany's dearest wish and dis-associated herself from those along whose side she had fought in the war, Wilson was certain that within twenty-five years the United States would have to fight Germany again at the side of the same allies and on the same battleground. This happened exactly twenty-five years after Wilson predicted it. He even fore-saw that the new German war would start by Germany's push eastwards against the small newly independent nations. The road to the east, he declared, was Germany's road to world domination. "If you do not close it," he insisted, "we have no choice but some day or other to enter into the same sort of war as we have just gone through."

By the 1930's the self-seeking nationalism and class egotism of the Western nations had undermined Western civilization to such a degree that twenty years after the first war Germany and Japan could start new hegemonical wars, despising modern civili-zation. Its cause seemed lost at the beginning of 1941, when the Communist and Fascist dictatorships of Stalin, Hitler, Mussolini and Franco apparently stood united in their opposition to West-ern liberalism. The whole European continent, with the exception of the two small enclaves of Switzerland and Sweden, was lost to liberty. Britain alone held out as an isolated and besieged island.

In the spring of 1941 the Japanese foreign minister Yosuke Matsuoka made an extended trip to Berlin and Rome and aligned his country more closely with the European Fascist axis. On his way back he stopped in Moscow where he was received with special courtesy and warmth by the Soviet government, with which he signed a five-year nonaggression and friendship pact on April 13. By breaking, a few months later, his pact with Stalin—as Stalin was later to break his pact with Japan—Hitler himself weakened the mortal threat to modern civilization presented by its united foes. The attack launched at the end of 1941 against the United States by Japan, knowing her rear secure by the treaty of friendship with Soviet Russia, as Hitler had known his rear secure by a similar treaty when he attacked the West the year before, forced this country to face the threat to the survival of liberty. The combined British and American efforts, after a long struggle, defeated Fascism, liberated much of Europe, though not the Iberian peninsula and eastern Europe, and provided a new chance for Western civilization.

X

WESTERN civilization which had reached its nadir in 1940 emerged strengthened from the Second World War. The major part of Germany, whose defection from the West had sparked the two wars, returned to the West. It ceased being a Roman or Prussian Reich and became a Federal Republic. Its center of gravity shifted from its northeastern borderlands to its western regions where it had been for most of German history. A new feeling of unity, consultation and cooperation bound the Western countries together, strengthened their morale, and helped to restore an unprecedented degree of well-being after the ravages of the war, a well-being shared, for the first time, by all classes of the population. Franco-German wars which for centuries had been an almost "normal" phenomenon of European history, became unthinkable. Though old national sentiments and rivalries continued among the North Atlantic nations, they were far below their former virulence and did not prevent a cooperation which if it had existed before 1939 might have prevented Fascist triumphs in Europe and which now succeeded in containing the Communist drive toward the Atlantic and the Mediterranean. The North American continent cooperated with Western Europe. The ocean had become a connecting link; the days of isolationism, so self-assertive in the 1920's and 1930's, were gone.

The North Atlantic Treaty Organization came into being in Washington, D.C. on April 5, 1949. At the signing of the pact, President Truman declared: "The nations represented here are bound together by the ties of long standing. We are joined by a common heritage of democracy, individual liberty, and the rule of law." The Belgian representative, Paul Henri Spaak, asserted that the "North Atlantic Pact is an act of faith in the destiny of Western civilization." And Ernest Bevin, signing on behalf of Great Britain, pointed out that "at last democracy is no longer a series of isolated units. It has become a cohesive organization, determined to fulfill its great purpose." The North Atlantic Treaty Organization was originally conceived as a defensive military pact of democracy against Communism. But in order to fulfill its purpose, it will have to transcend this narrow aim of an anti-Communist instrument, geared to military objectives. It can last only by conducting a positive struggle for a civilization of freedom and by raising it "to a level, where it will not be fought by arms alone, not even mainly by arms, but by intelligent insight into the need of world order, seen in the historical perspective of the growth of Western civilization."[10]

The North Atlantic Treaty Organization represents one of the many new frontiers in international relations opened up since World War II—the Truman Doctrine of March 1947, the Marshall Aid, European Unity, Common Market, Point Four Program—all of them pioneering ventures which before 1940 no one would have expected to materialize even in their present very

[10] This was written in 1949, in Hans Kohn, *The Twentieth Century* (New York: Macmillan, 1949), p. 234 (in the new enlarged edition of 1957 on p. 290). This point of view which stresses the cultural community and the message of universal liberty more than military considerations was expressed in the Conference on North Atlantic Community, which met in Bruges, Belgium, in September, 1957 under the joint auspices of the Foreign Policy Research Institute of the University of Pennsylvania and of the Collège d'Europe. See Ernst Bieri, "An Atlantic Dialogue in Bruges," and Hans Kohn, "The Atlantic Community and the World," in *Orbis. A quarterly journal of world affairs* (Philadelphia, Winter 1958), vol. I, no. 4.

imperfect form. Equally important has been the development within modern civilization itself, its awareness of liberty, equality and human dignity, which though inherent as a promise in modern civilization have only recently moved toward a wider realization. For the first time in history, the time-hallowed institutions like serfdom, crude exploitation of the economically or socially weaker classes and the subjection of one people to another have become unacceptable to the conscience of man and to public opinion.

In 1889, when, in celebration of the centenary of the French Revolution, the Second Socialist International was founded in Paris, the problem of labor in modern industrial society seemed insoluble. The proletariat regarded itself as an outsider, engaged in class-war against the capitalists who on their part showed no inclination to accept the worker as a partner in political and economic life. The task of the modern state, which emerged in the age of the Enlightenment, to emancipate and integrate all classes, castes, religions and ethnic groups on a footing of equality, and to intensify and speed up their assimilation in an open and fluid society, was not achieved even in the more developed countries of the West before 1914. Dr. Sun Yat-sen, after his visits to the United States, England and France, wrote in 1905 that "though the Western countries are powerful, their people are really in distress. Judging from the frequency of general strikes and the growth of anarchism and socialism, a social revolution is not far off." Lenin in 1918 could still hope for proletarian revolutions to break out in the advanced industrial societies as Marx had confidently predicted. But by the middle of the twentieth century modern Western society had put an end to the expectation of a workers' revolution. The formerly disinherited proletariat, exploited and insecure, is on the way to becoming a full and equal partner in modern Western society. Never has there been in history a change affecting the status and well-being of so many so fast as the transition from the conditions of Western workers around 1900 to those prevailing in 1960.[11]

[11] "The degree of satisfaction obtained by the worker is far more conditioned by his conception of the outside world and his place in it than by the possession or non-possession of the means of production." (L. Moulin, "The Curse of Ideologies," European Productivity, no. 37, Winter 1960, p. 45.)

After achieving the emancipation of the Western proletariat to equality and dignity, modern Western civilization is facing the greater and more difficult task of emancipating the peoples of the less developed countries, of whom many were until recently living in the status of subject populations, to a similar feeling of equality and dignity. This emancipation, a turning point in the history of mankind, inaugurates a new era in the relations among peoples, nationalities and races. For throughout history, peoples everywhere have subjected, oppressed or exterminated other peoples. Europeans did it as much, in Europe as well as in other continents, as did Asians or Africans. Only in recent times has modern Western civilization proclaimed the desirability of the emancipation and the equality of all peoples, and in the last decades peoples subjected to European or American rule have been set free in a way which half a century ago nobody would have thought possible. Imperialism and colonialism were not inventions of the modern West: they have been common to all races and times. But only modern Western civilization has finished by declaring them unacceptable. In the still-existing empires of the modern Western nations emancipation and equality are progressing at a rapid pace. Though ugly relics of the "old" spirit of domination persist, the pace and impact of the transformation are felt everywhere, and this transformation is the fruit of modern Western civilization.

For from the beginning this modern civilization has not been Western in any exclusive sense. The word "Western" means only that this civilization and its methods and institutions originated in the West, in northwestern Europe and in North America. But countries which geographically are Western countries, do not thereby alone form part of modern Western civilization. Fascist or Communist countries despise the spirit of Western liberty and reject its methods and institutions. On the other hand, the methods and institutions of modern Western civilization have spread far beyond the geographic area which may be called the West or the North Atlantic.

The West has spread its message, often unwittingly, by its existence and example, though it knows very well that it itself has

---

Social and psychological factors, the feeling of equality, personal dignity and freedom in work, are more powerful than purely economic factors.

not lived up to its own message. But its shortcomings are, to a certain degree, compensated by an inclination to a free and untrammeled self-criticism, which may sometimes even go too far, but which represents a safeguard on the one hand against smugness and stagnation, orthodoxy and dogmatism, and on the other hand against a dangerous utopianism and perfectionism. Being self-critical means to be conscious of the fact that no human society can approach perfection, and at the same time to be aware of the possibility and necessity of constant amelioration.

Stalin, Hitler and Mussolini were, at least as long as they were in power, regarded by their peoples and followers as embodiments of perfection, nay of infallibility. Modern Western civilization knows of no perfection. It knows only of its goal, which it approaches with great labor and yet toward which it has recently made greater progress than anybody could have believed in 1740 or in 1940. It is opposed to the rule of one man over another, of one class over another, of one people over another, of one religion over another, whatever the class, the people or the religion be. It rejects every form of exclusivism, and most sharply that practiced by peoples or governments which claim to share the principles of modern Western civilization. Its principles and institutions are, as we pointed out, of recent origin. They have not yet taken firm roots even in many European countries. Only in the twentieth century have they started to penetrate non-Western peoples and to exercise there, too, their liberating influence.

PART THREE

THE AGE OF PAN-NATIONALISM
THE GLOBAL AWAKENING OF PEOPLES

"In place of the old local and national seclusion and self-sufficiency, we have intercourse in every direction, universal interdependence of nations. And as in material, so also in intellectual production. The intellectual creations of individual nations become common property. . . . The bourgeoisie, by the rapid improvement of all instruments of production, by the immensely facilitated means of communication, draws all, even the most barbarian, nations into civilization. . . . It compels all nations . . . to introduce what it calls civilization into their midst. . . . In one word, it creates a world after its own image."

Marx and Engels,
The Communist Manifesto, 1848

"My spirit has pass'd in compassion and
   determination around the whole earth,
I have look'd for equals and lovers and found them
   ready for me in all lands,
I think some divine rapport has equallized me with
   them. . . .

Toward you all, in America's name,
I raise high the perpendicular hand, I make the
   signal. . . ."

Walt Whitman, *Salut au Monde!*

I

THE PROCESS of European penetration into non-European continents started in the fifteenth century and led to the discovery of the globe. It was made possible by the newly awakened dynamic spirit of Western Europe and thus formed the first step toward establishing European hegemony. Yet even at the time when the Hapsburg prince Charles V ruled over an expanding New World empire, the simultaneous advance of the Islamic Turks into the heart of central Europe and the Hapsburg dominions proved the relative weakness of the Western world. The first siege of Vienna by the Turks occurred in 1529; the Sultan rejected the offer of Ferdinand I, Charles V's brother, to pay tribute for Hungary in return for Turkish recognition of Hapsburg's rights there. For a century the Austrian Hapsburgs continued to pay tribute to the Sultan for the small fringe of Hungary left under their administration.[1]

Three centuries later, in 1855, Tocqueville wrote to Gobineau who was then on diplomatic service in Persia: "I am very curious to know to what you attribute the rapid and seemingly inevitable decadence of the races you have seen; a decadence which, as it already has delivered some, may deliver all of them to the domination of our little Europe, which so often trembled before them in the past. Where is the maggot that is eating this large Asian body? The Turks have become bad soldiers and now seem destined to be cheated and defeated by everybody. Yet you live now in the Mohammedan nation which, if the travelers' accounts are to be believed, is intelligent and even refined. What is this irredeemable decadence dragging it down through the centuries? Is it possible that we have risen while they remain static? I do not think so. I rather think that the dual movement has occurred in opposite directions. You say that one day we shall resemble your Eastern mobs: perhaps. But before that happens, we shall be

[1] See on the early period of European expansion J. H. Parry, *The Establishment of the European Hegemony; 1415–1715: Trade and Exploration in the Age of the Renaissance* (Harper Torchbooks, 1961).

their masters. A few million men who, a few centuries ago, lived nearly shelterless in the forests and in the marshes of Europe will, within a hundred years, have transformed the globe and dominated the other races. Seldom has Providence shown us an aspect of the future so clearly. European races are often the greatest rogues, but at least they are rogues to whom God gave will and power and whom he seems to have destined for some time to be at the head of mankind. Nothing on the entire globe will resist their influence."

In these sentences Tocqueville revealed his unusual sense of perspective. He knew that the superiority of the Europeans was temporary. He foresaw that Western civilization would transform the globe. The truly global expansion of Europe and European influence started only after Tocqueville had written these words. When Marx and Engels wrote in 1848 that Western civilization was re-forming all nations after its own image and when Tocqueville seven years later predicted that nothing on the globe would resist Western influence, the process had hardly started. The interior of Asia and Africa was then largely unknown. The heartlands of those continents were closed to Europeans. Only in the 1850's did David Livingstone cross the African continent for the first time. In the same decade India became a British crown colony. Central Asia was penetrated by the Russians in the 1860's, and only in the 1870's the first steps were taken to open up the Congo basin. About ten years later the French established their effective control over Indo-China. The period of European domination of Africa and Asia lasted, in many of its parts, less than a century. This brief duration of the age of European imperialism is not always realized. Yet in these few decades Africa and Asia were more completely and deeply transformed than in all preceding history.

The most powerful and most ancient Asian empire at the end of the eighteenth century was China. In the years 1794 and 1795 an embassy of the Dutch East India Company visited the Court of the Emperor of China. One of its leaders, A. E. Van-Braam Houckgeest, wrote in his account of the journey that "everything in China shows a complete ignorance of its inhabitants in regard to Europe, and they hear it spoken of with equal indifference.

The Emperor, as well as all those whom the public opinion places immediately next to him, think that they hold the first rank among all the created beings of this immense universe, and that they are at the head of the first nation to be found throughout the vast extent of space. A kind of miracle must be operated before the idea of sending a Chinese as an envoy to other nations can enter into a Chinese head." One year before, a British mission under Earl Macartney, who had been governor of Madras and became later governor of the Cape of Good Hope, was dispatched to Peking to try to improve trade with China and to establish diplomatic relations. The Emperor rejected both demands.

"As to your entreaty," the Imperial Mandate ran, "to send one of your nationals to be accredited to my Celestial Court and to be in control of your country's trade with China, this request is contrary to all usage of my dynasty and cannot possibly be entertained. . . . Your proposed envoy to my Court could not . . . be allowed liberty of movement and the privilege of corresponding with his own country; so that you would gain nothing by his residence in our midst. . . . As your ambassador can see for himself, we possess all things. I set no value on objects strange or ingenuous, and have no use for your country's manufactures. . . . It behoves you, O King, to respect my sentiments and to display even greater devotion and loyalty in future, so that, by perpetual submission to our Throne, you may secure peace and prosperity for your country hereafter."

A second mandate was even more outspoken in its rejection of all the concrete proposals submitted by the British: "Hitherto, all European nations, including your own country's barbarian merchants, have carried on their trade with our Celestial Empire at Canton . . . although we possess all things in prolific abundance. . . . But as the tea, silk and porcelain which the Celestial Empire produces, are absolute necessities to European nations . . . we have permitted, as a signal mark of favor, that foreign factories should be established at Canton, so that your wants might be supplied and your country thus participate in our beneficence. . . . Our dynasty, swaying the myriad races of the globe, extends the same benevolence towards all. . . . If other nations, following your bad example, wrongfully importune my ear with further impossible requests, how would it be possible for me to treat them with easy indulgence? Nevertheless, I do not forget the lonely remoteness of your island, cut off from the world by intervening wastes of sea, nor do I overlook your excusable ignorance of the usages of our Celestial Empire. I have consequently commanded my ministers to enlighten your ambassador on the subject and have ordered the departure of the mission."[2]

Only in 1842, after the first British-Chinese War, some of the demands made by Lord Macartney's mission were accepted by China and the process of opening China to intercourse with the West started, though very slowly and with continuing great resistance on the part of the Chinese. Japan entered into intercourse with the West two decades later, but Japanese reaction to the enforced opening of the country was entirely different from that of China. With a high degree of realism the leading statesmen advocated a break with the past "in order that strength might be derived from the new." Interestingly enough Japan was instrumental, only a decade after her own Westernization began, in opening contact with the secluded Kingdom of Korea (in 1876), after a similar American attempt, by landing Marines, had five years before been defeated. By the end of the nineteenth century the process, foreseen by Marx and Tocqueville, was well under way. The influence of Western civilization was beginning to penetrate to the far ends of the globe. By 1900 most of Asia and Africa was under direct or indirect European control. The partition of China seemed imminent and the formerly haughty empire had to accept the humiliating conditions of the Boxer Protocol of 1901. Only Japan, through Westernizing national reform, could participate herself in the imperialist drive and prepare the subjugation of Korea.[3]

[2] Harley Farnsworth MacNair, *The Real Conflict Between China and Japan* (The University of Chicago Press, 1938), pp. 22–38.

[3] Writing in 1935, Professor William L. Langer remarked that the last decade of the nineteenth and the first decade of the twentieth centuries will stand out as "the crucial epoch during which the nations of the Western world extended their political, economic and cultural influence over Africa and over large parts of Asia. The tide of European control has already turned and we are living now in an age of retreat and retirement. The tremendous outburst of expansion and the almost complete victory of Europe was, therefore, crowded into a couple of generations. . . ." *The Diplomacy of Imperialism, 1890–1902* (New York: Alfred A. Knopf, 1935), I, 67.

II

EUROPEAN penetration of the peoples of the globe at the turn of the century had a threefold impact upon them. It awakened them out of traditionalism and lethargy to the influence of modern civilization which thereby became the first universal civilization. By 1960 many of its aspects—general popular education, economic and social mobility, the emancipation of women, industrialization, public welfare—were accepted or desired everywhere. At the same time this civilization was imparted to them under the form of nationalism and imperialism, which by the turn of the century had become the dominant elements of Western public thought. "In every nation of Europe from England and France to Russia and Turkey," Gilbert Murray wrote in 1900 in the *International Journal of Ethics*, "in almost every nation in the world from the Americans to the Chinese and the Finns, the same whisper from below the threshold sounds incessantly in men's ears: We are the pick and flower of nations; the only nation that is really generous and brave and just. We are above all things qualified for governing others; we know how to keep them exactly in their place without weakness and without cruelty." This spread of Western civilization in the form of nationalism was instrumental in bringing, after only a brief duration, the era of European hegemony and imperialism to an end. Nationalism, until then confined to the Western peoples, rapidly became a universal phenomenon, the Age of Nationalism of the European nineteenth century passed almost imperceptibly into the Age of Pan-nationalism of the global twentieth century. The awakening of the non-Western peoples, which came about as the result of Western influence, found its expression in an emancipation from Western domination. This was the unexpected but inevitable consequence of the fact, that the idea of emancipation, of human liberty and equality, was deeply embedded in the stream of modern civilization which started in the West in the seventeenth and eighteenth centuries and now began to spread over the globe.

In the progress of modern Western civilization, the ruling classes, especially in the English-speaking countries, extended their privileges into rights for the underprivileged. In doing it they were moved by outside pressure but also by the nature of their civilization. Similarly the imperial Western nations, often reluctantly but also prompted from within, have been divesting themselves of imperial control. Gilbert Murray characterized the process in domestic affairs in words which, within limits, apply also to imperial affairs: "It was people who had the vote who worked to have the franchise given to the voteless; Christians who worked for the emancipation of the Jews; Protestants for the emancipation of the Catholics; members of the Church of England who abolished the Test Acts. The same with the legislation of trade unions, the abolition of slavery, the protection of native races—always a privileged class giving up its privileges on grounds of conscience or human principle." Murray may have overlooked other factors promoting this development, but without doubt in the Western liberal tradition (in which in the English-speaking countries the "conservatives" shared) the faith in human dignity and in the oneness of mankind was an important factor in effecting the emancipation of underprivileged groups. "Let the whole world be cleansed," Hawthorne wrote, "or not a man or woman of us can be clean." With nationalism as collective egotism being the most powerful force in late nineteenth- and early twentieth-century Europe, it was to a certain degree easier to desist from oppressing or degrading members of one's own national group than "outsiders." Egotism or conceit of nations—the chosen people idea—are more dangerous than the same vices applied to and by individuals. Nevertheless the process of the emancipation of Western dependencies was running its course in 1962 and Britain and France, shedding their imperial traditions which were still strong in 1945, were turning into purely European nations.[4]

In the heyday of imperialism in Europe and the United States, which lasted from the aftermath of Bismarck's triumphs on the battlefields to the aftermath of World War I, it was nationalist passion and prestige, competition and jealousy, much more than rational considerations of economic gain which prompted the rapid expansion of colonialism. Private interests and personal careers gained from it, as they do from warlike actions and organ-

[4] See on imperial policies A. P. Thornton, *The Imperial Idea and its Enemies. A Study in British Power* (London: Macmillan, 1959), and Rupert Emerson, *From Empire to Nation. The Rise to Self-Assertion of Asian and African Peoples* (Harvard University Press, 1960).

ized exploitation in general, and often gained most handsomely. But nations as such did not prosper on account of expansion. When Germany, the Netherlands and Britain lost their colonial Empires, the national economy not only did not suffer from it but was able to provide a higher standard of living for the majority of its citizens than they had known in "imperial" days. But though economic considerations play a great role in the calculations of corporations and in the subconscious motivations of individuals, the historian will find that throughout the age of modern nationalism and imperialism (the two are closely intertwined and often indistinguishable) national feeling and aspirations have taken precedence over rational considerations of economic gain.[5]

At the end of World War I Western imperialism seemed firmly in the saddle. Perhaps few documents are as characteristic of the spirit of imperialism in its heyday as the Sykes-Picot Treaty of 1916 dividing Middle Eastern lands among the presumptive victors, and the subsequent disposition of Arab lands to non-Arab interests. The similar partition of the Anatolian homeland of the Turks was prevented by the victory of the forces of Mustafa Kemal over the invading Greeks who tried to re-establish the Hellenic empire of antiquity. Kemal's success, made possible by his treaty of friendship with Lenin's Soviet Russia, which at that time sharply reversed the former Russian imperialist policy of expansion into Turkey, marked a milestone in the beginning of the process of "decolonization" and of the nationalist Westernization and mobilization of a region which only a few decades before had been known for its picturesque medievalism and Oriental stagnation.

World War I stimulated nationalism throughout Asia and Africa, as it did in Europe itself. It took several decades and the effect of World War II before nationalism became an effective force in the two former continents (and in Latin America), but in Europe it continued to manifest itself, even after World War

[5] See Henri Brunschvig, *Mythes et réalités de l'impérialisme colonial français, 1871–1914* (Paris: Colin, 1960). Of older German studies see Walter Sulzbach, *Nationales Gemeinschaftsgefühl und wirtschaftliches Interesse* (Leipzig, 1929) and Arthur Salz, *Das Wesen des Imperialismus* (Leipzig, 1931).

I, in colonial ambitions. The rivalry of Britain and France for imperial control of Middle-Eastern lands grew in intensity after 1918. Weak European nations like Italy and even Poland dreamed of colonial acquisition. In discussing the future of colonialism even as late as 1938 the chief problem in the mind of European statesmen was not the process of decolonization but the return of former German colonies to Germany. In the Labor government's declaration of policy on August 22, 1945 no mention was made of independence for the colonies. The rapid development of the following fifteen years came as a surprise. Yet in Asia and Africa Westernization and nationalism had been growing since the last decades of the nineteenth century in breadth and depth, a parallel development to the intensification of European imperialism.

III

THE TWO countries in Africa and Asia in which, through a closer contact with Europe, modern nationalism first spread were Egypt and India. The lower Nile valley reasserted its historical role. Seat of the oldest civilization, it had later been the home of Hellenism and then the geographic and intellectual center of the Islamic world. The eighteenth century recognized its strategic value on the road to India and Napoleon Buonaparte invaded it in 1798. He brought with him the Revolution's administrative reforms and scholarly investigations. Under their inspiration two developments set in: by 1811 an Albanian soldier of fortune, Mohammed Ali, had become Egypt's undisputed ruler; a man of great energy, comparable to Peter the Great, he sent young Egyptians as students abroad and with the help of French instructors built a modern army and navy, reintroduced Egypt into Middle Eastern and European politics as an active and powerful factor and hoped to make it the center of an Islamic renaissance. At the same time the nucleus of an incipient modern intelligentsia tried not only to popularize European science but to revive Arabic culture and reform Egyptian society. The rediscovery, by European scholars, of the great Pharaonic and Arabic past of the country stimulated a sense of national pride and the rise of an Egyptian nationalism.

The opening of the Suez Canal in 1869; the growing wealth and

extravagance with its concomitant budgetary disorder which led
to a joint Franco-British financial control; the establishment of
the first modern nationalist organization, the al-hizb al-watani, the
Party of the Fatherland, which was no longer based on religion
but accepted Egyptian Mohammedans, Christians and Jews alike
("We are all brothers in this land and must have equal political
rights"); the introduction of a popular free press and political
agitation; the convocation of a Chamber of Deputies—these
changes supplied the background of a liberal spirit which expressed itself in the first nationalist revolution under Ahmed Arabi
in 1879 and in the evolutionary Islamic reform movement of
Mohammed Abdu. One of the few officers of Egyptian fellah
(peasant) stock, Arabi opposed both: the corrupt rule of the
Turkish landowning aristocracy and foreign control and interference in the country. Characteristic of the new assertion of
dignity was the answer which Arabi gave in 1881 to Khedive
Tewfiq, the descendant of Mohammed Ali, who then ruled Egypt
and said "I am the Khedive and shall do as I please." To this
Arabi replied: "We are not slaves and shall never from this day on
be inherited." He hoped to break the oppressive rule of the
Turkish-Albanian ruling class and of the grasping foreign interests
and to turn Egypt into a constitutional republic. He was defeated
by native inertia and British interference. A British expeditionary
force occupied the country in 1882. The time for the realization
of Arabi's hopes came only seventy years later.[6]

The British occupation in its typical makeshift and compromise
preserved the outward forms of Egyptian statehood with indigenous administrative and consultative bodies; it declared the training of the Egyptians in liberal self-government as its goal. Though
this remained, in practice, a very distant goal, the British occupation brought Egypt in closer touch with European thought and

[6] Lord Cromer, the British pro-consul in Egypt from 1884 to 1907, wrote
in his report in 1905 that Arabi's movement "was, in its essence, a genuine
revolt against misgovernment," and "was not essentially anti-European." See
on the early nationalism of Egypt Jamal Mohammed Ahmad, The Intellectual Origins of Egyptian Nationalism (Oxford University Press, 1960);
Wilfrid Scawen Blunt, Secret History of the English Occupation of Egypt
(London: T. Fisher Unwin, 1907); Hans Kohn, A History of Nationalism
in the East, tr. from the German (London: Routledge and Sons, 1929), pp.
174–221 and bibliography, pp. 442–444.

produced a gradual change in social institutions and habits of life. Egypt became the most advanced Islamic country; the improved judicial order, the more secure and broader liberty, the growing economic prosperity induced many Arab nationalists from Syria, Mohammedans and Christians, to settle in Cairo or to publish their writings there, unhindered by the censorship of the Turkish government. Cairo became more and more the intellectual center of the Arab-speaking world, but the national movement in the Nile valley regarded itself, in spite of close cultural ties, not as Arabic but as Egyptian. Nor did Arabs and Egyptians face then the same "enemy." From 1882 to 1918 the Arabs of Syria and Iraq fought Turkish domination, whereas the Egyptians struggled to end the British occupation.

These years were filled in Egypt with an attempt to reform Islam and to bring it into line with modern civilization. The leading figure in this movement was Mohammed Abdu who wished to see a transformation of the mind and heart of Egyptian society and thereby to equip it for freedom. Together with his friends and followers—among whom was Saad Zaghlul, who became the venerated leader of Egyptian nationalism from 1918 to 1927—Abdu established the Muslim Benevolent Society and the Society for the Revival of Arabic Books. Lord Cromer called Abdu and his followers "the Girondists of the Egyptian national movement." The most active among them were Ahmed Fathi Zaghlul, Saad's brother, Qasim Amin and Ahmed Lutfi al-Sayyid. Among many other books they translated Rousseau and Bentham and were strongly influenced by John Stuart Mill. They hoped to endow the Egyptians with a new feeling of dignity, to teach them the rights of the individual in and against society, and to combat the age-old lethargy. "With Muslims, determinism has come to stay and has gradually suppressed action," one of the reformers wrote. "Faith has deteriorated into a negation of reason. They call indolence trust in God and the search for truth heresy. For them this is religion, and anyone who holds different views is exposed to abuse. . . . Unquestioning acceptance of everything old is with them the heart of wisdom."

Qasim Amin was the most outspoken among the reformers. His writings on "The Emancipation of Women" and "The New Woman" produced heated discussions. He warned that holding on to a petrified past was inviting disaster. Those who regarded the West as an implacable enemy were in his opinion not really helping Egypt, for Europe had to teach the East not only its industrial civilization but that art which was the key to all others—civic virtues, then almost unknown in the East. The social and intellectual revolution which was under way, both by the increased contact with Europe and by the writings of the reformers, was helped by the educational reforms which Saad Zaghlul as minister of education initiated before World War I. He laid great stress on Arab literature and in 1908 the first university, supported by voluntary contributions, was founded with 754 students, among whom thirty-one were women.

None emphasized more strongly than Lutfi the need for raising the intellectual and moral character of the Egyptian people. Though the British occupation had introduced the foundations of personal freedom and equal rights before the law, the Egyptians had not yet learned to look on the government as an instrument for serving them. Political emancipation from the British was not enough; the Egyptian character had to change. Lutfi knew that this presented all underdeveloped lands with the more difficult task. "The newspapers expose the faults of Britain but refrain from exposing the inner forces of decay within the Egyptian people themselves. Britain could be attacked because her power was not sanctified by a religion or a tradition, but the forces of local authority were protected from criticism by a system of habit which itself had acquired something of the sanctity of religion." Egypt had to accept not only the paraphernalia, but the principles of modern civilization, which in recent times had changed Europe and established European hegemony. Only with the help of these principles could true progress in Egypt be achieved. By assimilating the best from European civilization, Egypt would not lose but strengthen her identity, Lutfi argued. In their creative period the Arabs had assimilated the civilizations with which they had come into contact; in a similar way Egypt had to assimilate besides European science and technology the philosophical ideas which had made this progress possible. "The wave of civilization has come to us with all its virtues and vices, and we must accept it without resisting it. All that we can do is to Egyptianize the good that it carries and narrow down the channels through which the evil can run. We must possess that civilization as it is but try to control it."[7]

Political nationalism before World War I, which had not a Girondist but a Jacobin temper, was led by Mustapha Kamil who until 1904 looked to France for cooperation and inspiration; after the Anglo-French Entente Cordiale of that year he looked to Japan, whose advent on the stage of international politics he greeted with the book "The Rising Sun" (1904). In 1896 he had written: "Egyptian civilization will last only if it is rooted in the people, if the fellah, the merchant, the teacher, the student, in short every Egyptian knows that man possesses sacred and inviolable rights, that he was not created to be a tool but to lead an honorable and reasonable life, that no sentiment is more beautiful than the love of our country, that the soul is noble, and a people without independence is a people without existence. Patriotism speedily raises backward peoples to civilization, greatness and power. Patriotism is the blood that flows in the veins of virile nations and that gives life to all living creatures." Egyptian political nationalism around the turn of the century clearly used the current phraseology of European nationalism. Similarly Hamed el Alaily emphasized that "the curse of the imitation of a superior foreign class destroys all springs of real life among the people. The nation then becomes only an intellectual parasite . . . and ceases to contribute anything of its own to the moral and intellectual life of humanity." Mustapha Kamil caught the imagination of the urban middle class and masses; he died while still a young man and his funeral in Cairo in 1908 became a great nationalist demonstration; it was, in the words of an English observer, "one of the most impressive sights ever witnessed in Cairo in modern times."[8]

[7] Jamal Mohammed Ahmed, The Intellectual Origins of Egyptian Nationalism, op. cit., pp. 86–112. "For Lutfi national independence was not an end; he was concerned above all with the quality of national life, with the virtues it generated. The first of these virtues was freedom. There is no need to summarize his views on liberty, because they were those of Locke and Mill." Mr. Ahmed's book is the best introduction to an understanding of the growth of Egyptian nationalism, and of Asian nationalism in general before 1914. The author is a Sudanese scholar and diplomat.
[8] Moustafa Kamil, Egyptiens et Anglais (Paris: Perrin et Cie., 1906); Hamid el Alaily, The Future of Egypt; The Moral and Intellectual Aspects of Egyptian Nationalism (Speech at the Egyptian National Congress at Brus-

After 1907, the denunciation of British rule was not only voiced in mass meetings and popular oratory but also, though in less rhetorical terms, in the Legislative Assembly. In 1910 Egypt seemed to the Egyptian patriots farther away from self-government than it had been before the British occupation. "In 1884 we imported flour to a value of £ 134,000, in 1909 to that of £ 1,836,000," one of them observed. "Under Mohammed Ali we sent 905 students to Europe, under Ismail we sent 155, [now] we are sending 43. What is the remedy? Self-government! And for the last thirty years we have not moved one inch towards self-government."[9]

Then in the wake of World War I a great and sudden step towards self-government was taken in Egypt as it was throughout Europe. It was spurred by the nationalist excitement produced everywhere by the long duration and the bitterness of the struggle and by the promises of national self-determination made during the war by the United States and by Britain. To weaken Turkey, the latter supported the rise and revolt of an Arab national movement within the Turkish empire in the Hejaz, where the holy cities of Islam, Mecca and Medina, were located, and in the lands of the Fertile Crescent surrounding the peninsula in the north in an arc stretching from the Persian Gulf to the Sinai peninsula, where Damascus, Beirut and Baghdad had been for some time centers of nationalist agitation. As early as 1914 a leading German Islamic scholar had noticed the strength of Arab nationalism among the various princely and local ambitions in the Arabic speaking parts of Turkey: "It is obvious that all these various centrifugal elements can nowhere find support among the Arab people for their particularist interests. They must therefore hide them under the cover of an idea of great attractive power. That is the idea of Arab nationalism. The very fact that it is being chosen as the most effective cover proves that it has a great attraction and that there exists in the widest circles an Arab national sentiment which can unite the people across the barriers of religious creeds. The age of a conscious nationalism has arrived in the Arab East, not only for the most advanced parts but for

---

sels, 21st to 24th September, 1910; Paris: 1910); J. Alexander, *The Truth about Egypt* (London: Cassell, 1911), p. 139.

[9] George Young, *Egypt* (London: Ernest Benn, 1927), p. 191.

the whole Arabic-speaking area. The fact that even the autocratic princes of [the northern part of the Arabian peninsula] support the thought of a union of the Arab lands, perhaps in the form of a federation, proves that the consciousness of an Arab nation is already penetrating into the peninsula. And that plainly means that the solution of the territorial problems of these lands, which on account of their strategic position threaten to be of world political concern, can no longer be solved from the point of view of the great powers but only within the framework of the Arab national program as a whole."[10]

The fact of the penetration of nationalism into all Arab lands was not taken into consideration in the peace settlements of 1919–20. Thereupon revolts broke out in Egypt and Iraq, in Syria and Palestine. Only in Egypt had the national movement so far progressed in the years before World War I that it was able to take the first steps towards the realization of its aspirations. It possessed in Saad Zaghlul a mouthpiece honored by his own people and recognized internationally. For the first time the Arab urban middle classes were firmly united with the fellaheen in a common cause. For the first time, too, the Christian Copts fraternized with the Mohammedans, and Egyptian women were aroused to political activity. When Britain sent a commission under Lord Milner "to inquire into the cause of the late disturbances in Egypt," and when Balfour declared in the House of Commons (on November 17, 1919) that "British supremacy is going to be maintained" in Egypt, the Egyptian people reacted in unexpected unity. They resolved to boycott the Milner mission; the boycott was carried out with surprising discipline in towns and villages alike.

The British High Commissioner in Egypt, Fieldmarshal Viscount Allenby, forced concessions from the British government. As a result England granted in February, 1922 Egyptian independence, though in an imperfect and hesitant manner and with a number of important reservations subject to later negotiations. Yet it was the first step taken on the road to decolonization, achieved by the determination and unity of the people and the

[10] See Richard Hartman, "Die arabische Frage und das türkische Reich," in *Beiträge zur Kenntnis des Orients,* Jahrbücher der Deutschen Vorderasien Gesellschaft, vol. XV (Halle a.d.S.: Gebauer-Schwetscke, 1919).

liberal spirit of a British soldier. But for the next thirty years the course of Egyptian independence was unhappy and depressing. The British were slow and reluctant to relinquish their hold on the country; the native ruler, King Fuad who had been put on the throne by the British, was opposed to any democratization of Egyptian life; under the twofold burden of the policies of the British and of the Palace, Egyptian educated public opinion succumbed to a feeling of frustration and disillusion. Under the cloak of an official but unreal independence corruption from within and manipulation from without grew, as it did also in some Latin-American countries of the period.[11]

This situation changed thirty years after the grant of independence and seventy years after Arabi's defeat by the British. Arabi's ideals, premature and immature in his time, were brought nearer realization, when on July 23, 1952 a group of young officers overthrew the Turkish-Albanian monarchy and court aristocracy and gave the fellaheen the feeling of an active share in the government of their country. On January 23, 1953 the then leader of the revolution, General Mohammed Neguib, repeated Arabi's words: "We are no longer slaves, and never again shall we be passed on from father to son." During the Suez crisis of 1956 Gamal Abdel Nasser rallied the people as no Egyptian leader could do before his time. This new attitude was prepared by some young writers like Khalid Mohammed Khalid, a product of the reorganized El Azhar Theological School, who began to publish in 1950 stirring books with characteristic titles like "Here we begin" and "Citizens and not Subjects." He denounced not only religious and social backwardness, but also the way in which democratic institutions had been abused for the benefit of the wealthy and the ambitions of politicians. "Liberty is labor and toil," he wrote, "it is perseverance, vision and sincerity." A new hope and a new feeling of dignity replaced the pessimism of the preceding decades. Poverty and degradation, which had been the lot of the poorer classes in Egypt, as everywhere in Asia and Africa, since time immemorial, were no longer accepted; the firm conviction

---

[11] See Arnold J. Toynbee, *The Islamic World Since the Peace Settlement* (Survey of International Affairs, 1925, vol. I, London: Oxford University Press, 1927), pp. 195, 212, 226, and Hans Kohn, *Nationalism and Imperialism in the Hither East* (London: Routledge and Sons, 1932), chs. V–IX. tr. from the German.

grew that they can be overcome. The age of emancipation which had come to Europe in the eighteenth century dawned now for Egypt.[12]

The various nationalist movements in the Arab-speaking lands grew closer together, and after the establishment of the state of Israel Egyptian nationalism fused with other Arab movements for independence into one broad though diversified front. As it was the case with some national movements in nineteenth-century Europe, Arab nationalism, too, has to overcome deep-rooted differences of religion, social structure, geographic distance and vested regional interests. The Arab cultural renaissance, the spread of education, Egypt's advance in reforms and in international stature—all that gave a great impetus to a development which started with the formation of the Arab League by seven Arab states in Cairo on March 22, 1945. In the following years after attaining their independence, Libya, the Sudan, Morocco, Tunisia and Kuwait joined the League.

The progress in Arab unity can be best measured by recalling a statement, made as recently as 1939 by a historian of the Arab national movement. According to him the British occupation of Egypt at a time when the national awakening there had already begun to translate itself into a politically-minded movement, produced a new current of ideas whose inspiration was specifically Egyptian. "There was still, as there is today, a great deal of common ground as between Egyptian and Arab aspirations. But in the field of specific nationalist activity the disseverance was complete. The same applied to Tunisia in its subjection to a French protectorate. To a greater degree than ever before, the Arab national movement was finding itself confined to Syria, Iraq and the Arabian Peninsula." That was the judgment in 1939 of a leading Christian Syrian nationalist who had personal ties with Egypt. Any Moroccan participation in an Arab national movement was not even mentioned in 1939.[13]

When the Arab League was formed, North Africa outside

[12] See Wilson Wynn, Nasser of Egypt, The Search for Dignity, Introduction by Louis Lyons (Cambridge, Mass.: Arlington Books, 1959); Keith Wheelock, Nasser's New Egypt (New York: Praeger, 1960); Dana Adams Schmidt in The New York Times, Dec. 29, 1959.

[13] George Antonius, The Arab Awakening. The Story of the Arab National Movement (Philadelphia: Lippincott, 1939), p. 100.

Egypt took no part in it. It thus came as a surprise when the then Sultan of Morocco on the occasion of his first visit to Tangiers, then an international city, on April 10, 1947, praised the Arab League for enforcing bonds between all Arabs, "which has permitted their kings and leaders in the east and in the west to unify their will and march towards a moral progress." "It goes without saying," he declared two days later, in an interview with foreign journalists, "that Morocco, being a country attached by solid bonds to the Arab countries of the east, desires to strengthen those bonds even more resolutely, especially since the Arab League has now become an important factor in world affairs." In the Pact of Tangiers of April 9, 1951, the various factions of Moroccan nationalism in the French and Spanish zones of their country united in a national front and proclaimed cooperation with the Arab League to be "a national duty before and after realization of independence." Eight years later, Moroccan independence achieved, the Arab League held its annual meeting in Casablanca; Iraq and Tunisia were absent on account of intra-Arab dissensions. But at the meeting in Baghdad, the Iraqi capital, early in 1961, the foreign ministers of all member-states of the Arab League participated to coordinate Arab policies, especially with regard to Algeria and Palestine. Though no unified or federated Arab state is in sight for any foreseeable future—too great are the still-continuing local differences—an ever-closer cultural, political, economic and military cooperation, respecting the existing diversities, may be ahead far beyond anything expected in 1939.

IV

INDIA is less of a nation than the Arabs are. It possesses a similar cultural unity and a similarly common past. But there exist much greater racial and religious tensions in India, sharper divisions by caste, the lack of a common tongue and the jealousy of the many literary languages which have become the vehicle of cultural aspirations. Yet India, thanks to a British administration of 150 years, has been equipped with a unifying administrative structure and system of communications, lacking among the Arab lands, with the memory of a common struggle for independence, and above all with the common traditions of highly trained and

Westernized civil servants who for almost a century dedicated themselves to the task of building a modern nation.

India came in closer contact with Europe about the same time as Egypt did. But she lacked the unified state-character which Egypt possessed. India was deeply split into a great number of principalities and of conflicting religions and castes, leading an independent and separate life. It was dominated by the unmitigated grip of orthodox traditionalism. The first to break it was Ram Mohan Roy, a Bengali Brahmin, who studied Islam and Christianity and who came under the spell of humanist rationalism. He was the first Indian to favor social reform, to found a vernacular press, to advocate English education, and the first Hindu to break with caste rigidity by sailing for Europe. He died while traveling in England in 1833. The small religious society called Brahma Samaj which he founded with some other high-class Bengali Brahmins (among them Dwarkanath Tagore, the grandfather of the Bengali poet Rabindranath Tagore, the first Indian recipient of the Nobel Prize for literature in 1913) had as its ideal a union of the best in Asian and in European civilization. Some of his disciples founded a "Society for the Acquisition of General Knowledge" and issued a journal entitled "The Search for Knowledge."

Ram Mohan Roy gave the initial impulse towards the rebirth of India; he was the first to break through the complete seclusion of Hinduism and to dare to open avenues to its self-examination and self-criticism. "The chief value of [his] labors, to our mind," wrote an Indian nationalist at the beginning of the present century, "seems to lie in his fight against the forces of mediaevalism in India, and it is for this reason that we claim for him the honor of being the Father of the present Indian renaissance."[14] When the Medical College was opened in Calcutta in 1835 there were already a few high-caste Hindus who touched and dissected corpses in spite of the fact that this was strictly forbidden by their religion. In the same year Thomas Macaulay presented, as Chairman of the Committee of Public Instruction, his memorandum on Indian education. He advocated freedom of the press and equality of Europeans and Indians before the law. More im-

[14] Bepin Chandra Pal, The New Spirit (Calcutta: Sinha, Sarvadhikari and Co., 1907), p. 52.

portant, even, he proposed a system of modern education, based upon English culture and language. His intention in so doing was well expressed in his own words: "It may be that the public mind of India may so expand under our own system that it may outgrow that system, and our subjects having been brought up under good government may develop a capacity for better government, that having been instructed in European learning, they may crave for European institutions. I know not whether such a day will ever come, but if it does come it will be the proudest day in the annals of England."

The educated Indians, the product of these educational reforms and of the founding of many schools and colleges, became the fathers of Indian nationalism. "They have imbibed the ideas which we ourselves have set before them," the Montagu-Chelmsford Report on Constitutional Reforms in India, issued in 1918, stated in Article 139, "and we ought to reckon it to their credit. The present intellectual and moral stir in India is no reproach but rather a tribute to our work. . . . We owe [the educated Indian] sympathy because he has conceived and pursued the idea of managing his own affairs, an aim which no Englishman can fail to respect. . . . He has by speeches and in the press done much to spread the idea of a united and self-respecting India among thousands who had no such conception in their minds." India soon was in the vanguard among Asian nations in adapting Western political reforms and in following the British legal and constitutional model. The intercourse with Europe was far advanced by the time of World War I. In 1923 the English Universities counted among their students 1,401 from Asia (among whom 1,094 from India and Ceylon) and 1,171 from Africa (among whom 298 from Egypt). The Indian Mohammedans were slower in accepting Western influences than the Hindus. Sir Syed Ahmed Khan was the first among them to believe in the need for modern education. In 1869 he visited England and left his older son there to study in Cambridge: after his return he published a paper, "Mohammedan Social Reformer," which tried to disseminate and encourage modern education among his co-religionists. In 1877 he founded the Anglo-Oriental College in Aligarh.

The new generation of Indians educated in English ways laid

the foundation for the growth of an Indian nation by establishing the Indian National Congress which held the first of its annual meetings in Bombay at the end of 1885. With it the first free representative assembly and mouthpiece of public opinion in the history of Asia came into being. At least in theory the Congress stood for the whole of India, above race and caste, religion and province. Though the vast majority of its members were Hindus, between 1885 and 1914 three Mohammedans, four Englishmen and one Parsee were elected Presidents of the Congress, one Englishman twice and the Parsee three times. The Congress, first suggested by Allen Octavian Hume, an English liberal and former member of the Indian Civil Service, was to merge into one national whole all the different and hitherto hostile elements that make up the population of India; to direct the process of rebirth of the nation thus evolved, intellectually, morally, socially, and politically; and to strengthen the tie that binds Britain and India by changing whatever was unjust or injurious to India. The Congress was to bring the leaders of the various parts of India together, to arouse their feeling of unity, and to train them politically. The Congress met, for this purpose, every year in another city.

The leaders of the Congress before 1905 came from a generation raised in the outlook of British liberalism, of Mill and Gladstone. Among them were great personalities like Surendra Nath Banerjee and Gopal Krishna Gokhale. But at the turn of the century, following therein again the general trend of Western development, Indian nationalism became more self-centered, impatient and eager for action. Religious movements inspired by Dayananda, Ramakrishna and Vivekananda roused the pride of the youth in ancient Indian civilization and its faith in India's unique mission. They exhorted the people to steep their souls in the inherited wealth of Indian thought and to turn away from a West, held guilty of shallowness and materialism. The ancient gods were called upon and entreated to drive out the alien powers which were believed sapping India's very marrow. The youth formed secret societies and demanded deeds. As in other European and Asian countries, the students were often the heart and soul of this movement. Their leader was Bal Gandakar Tilak, a Chitpavan Brahmin, a caste which had ruled the great Maratha empire, established in the seventeenth century in the struggle against the Mohammedans. He wished to arouse a militant and military spirit in India and turned against the trend of social reform. In 1905 he tried to win the majority in the Congress. At its session in 1906 the Congress accepted the program of *swadeshi*, the boycott of English in favor of native products and material, and demanded for the first time self-government for India within the British Empire. But in the following year the British government introduced constitutional reforms in India and the moderates prevailed in the Congress.[15]

The First World War acted as a powerful leaven for nationalism in India as it did in Egypt. In both countries the masses began to become politically conscious. Elementary education spread among them; the position of women in public life underwent a gradual change; an incipient industrialization and an accelerated urbanization made their influence felt. Tilak and a remarkable English woman, Mrs. Annie Besant, who was then almost seventy years old and as the leader of the theosophist movement had made India her home, founded in 1916 the Indian Home Rule League. She was elected President of the Indian National Congress which met in December 1917 in Calcutta. The Congress rejected the constitutional reforms proposed for India by Britain in May 1918 as insufficient and opposed the intention of retaining the wartime regulations for combatting revolutionary and subversive agitation. But soon the Congress became even more radical. The generation which had guided the movement in late Victorian days disappeared from the stage; Mrs. Besant went over to the moderates; Tilak died in 1920. By then the Congress and the awakening masses had found a new leader in Mohandas Karamchand Gandhi, who only in 1914, at the age of forty-five, after many years of absence in London and South Africa, had returned to India. His main achievement lay, as did Saad Zaghlul's, in cementing the union of the urban middle class and the villagers. Gandhi revived the *swadeshi* movement and converted all sections of the Congress to the demand of *swaraj*, self-government. At the same time he became the leading voice in rejecting the "materialist" civilization of the modern West. India must not tread the

---

[15] An excellent analysis of the mood of the nationalist youth of this period is in Nirad C. Chaudhuri, *The Autobiography of an Unknown Indian* (New York: Macmillan, 1951), pp. 218 ff. and 391 ff.

path which had led Europe into the Great War.

The mood of the immediate postwar years can be best illus-
trated in the experience of a young Indian intellectual who later
became highly critical of Gandhi and of the extremism of Indian
nationalism. In 1920 he read in *The Times Literary Supplement*
a review of Oswald Spengler's *Der Untergang des Abendlandes.*
"There had been no second occasion in my life when the reading
of a mere review became so exultant an experience. . . . The thesis
of the book . . . agreed even more closely with my mood than
with the mood of a war-weary and disillusioned Europe. . . . The
pride and power of Europe which had inflicted such injury and
humiliation on us and which yet appeared so triumphant and
irresistible was going to be fought by something infinitely more
potent than our will and capacity: it was to be crushed by history
in its inexorable sweep."[16]

Gandhism led to a revival of a self-centered Hindu nationalism,
different from Ram Mohun Roy's early patriotism. Indian nationalists venerated and used Gandhi; but the India which emerged
went its own ways. The Hindu revival led to a new bitter anti-
Mohammedan feeling. Before and during World War II men like
the Cambridge-educated revolutionary, Subhas Chandra Bose,
captivated the imagination and aroused the loyalty of many
Indians. He became a hero to the masses as well as to the educated.
He led the extreme, terrorist wing of the nationalists and had a
Fascist-like preference for paramilitary formation and uniforms.
He separated from Gandhi, convinced, as he wrote in 1934, that
"India's salvation will not be achieved under his leadership." He
supported Britain's enemies, National Socialist Germany and
imperial Japan, and organized an "Indian National Army" to
invade India together with the Japanese. After his death in 1945
he became a legend in India, above all in Bengal, where pictures
of him were displayed in many homes.

But the independence came neither through Bose nor by Fascist victory. Independence was already foreshadowed in the Government of India Act of 1935 which laid the foundations for an
orderly transition to a self-governing democracy, and in Sir Staf-

---

[16] Nirad C. Chaudhuri, *op. cit.,* p. 397. See also pp. 400–433, a remarkable criticism on the atavistic Hindu character of Gandhi's nationalism and
its opposition to the liberal nationalism of the generation of 1885.

ford Cripps' mission to India in 1942. The Indianization of the higher services, civilian and military, began after World War I. In 1918 Indians were admitted to the Royal Military Academy in Sandhurst, England, and in 1934 an Indian Sandhurst was opened. The Indian army, a volunteer force, which consisted in 1939 of 189,000 men with 1,115 commissioned Indian officers, expanded during the War to 2,500,000 men with 15,740 Indian officers and, together with a Royal Indian navy and Royal Indian air force, rendered invaluable service to the British war effort in all theaters of the war. Even greater was India's economic contribution which spurred the industrial development of the country and turned it from a debtor into a creditor nation with large accumulated balances in London at the end of the War.

In June 1943 Field Marshal Viscount Wavell became Viceroy. He had been Allenby's aide in World War I; in World War II he was Allenby's successor as commander of the British armies in the Middle East and was transferred in 1941 to the post of commander of the British forces in India. He repeated in India what Allenby had done in Egypt.[17] With the end of World War II elections were held in India, and soon in all provinces responsible parliamentary ministries were again functioning. In February, 1946 the British prime minister Clement Attlee promised that India was free to decide on complete independence, including the right to leave the Commonwealth. An interim government, in which all portfolios were held by Indians, was set up, with Jawaharlal Nehru as vice-president to the Viceroy. The only obstacle now was the bitter feud between Hindus and Mohammedans, a feud based upon their different ways of life, their longstanding sentiments of distrust and resentment, and intensified by the growing aggressiveness and self-centeredness of Indian nationalism. In March, 1947 Viscount Mountbatten followed Lord Wavell as viceroy; the division of India into two sovereign states, India and Pakistan, was decided; and the British government introduced the India Independence Bill into the British parliament in July, 1947. It became law two weeks later. India became

---

[17] See Wavell's biography, *Allenby in Egypt* (New York: Oxford University Press, 1944), where he stressed Allenby's role in getting, against the wishes of the British cabinet, headed then by Lloyd George, the declaration of independence for Egypt.

independent on August 15, 1947. Both new states decided voluntarily to remain in the Commonwealth and British tradition lived
on in the civil service, the judiciary and the armed forces. Gandhi
was assassinated by a Hindu nationalist fanatic in January, 1948.

The grant of independence to India marked the most momen-
tous step in the history of decolonization. British India had been
the most conspicuous symbol of European imperial power. Theodore Roosevelt wrote on August 11, 1899, to Cecil Spring-Rice, a
British diplomat then in Teheran: "You have done such marvelous things in India that it may be that you will gradually as
century succeeds century, by keeping your hold transform the
Indian population not in blood, probably not in speech, but in
government and in culture, and thus leave your impress as Rome
did hers on Western Europe." It took not centuries, but less than
half a century for Britain to release its hold on India. India's
freedom became the signal for the rapid success of other nationalist struggles for independence in Asia and Africa. Most of the
new nations were less prepared for an orderly transition than
Egypt and India were, where modern nationalism went about as
far back as among many European peoples, who, like the Balkan
or Baltic peoples, began to experience the impact of Western
thought in the nineteenth century and were roused by it into
cultural and political activity. For most peoples in Asia and Africa
the years 1904–05 marked a turning point and a new beginning,
comparable therein to the years of 1848–49 in the history of central European nationalism.[18] In 1905, events connected with Russia
began to stir the peoples of Asia and Africa; for the first time the
influence of Russia took its place beside that of Britain, France
and the West in general.

V

THE RUSSIAN-JAPANESE War of 1904 and the abortive
Russian Revolution of 1905 marked a turning point in the history
of nationalism in Asia and Africa, and thereby in the history of
decolonization. Before the turn of the century the youth of Asia
and Africa had started to receive with enthusiasm the Western

[18] See Hans Kohn, *The Twentieth Century* (New edition, New York:
Macmillan, 1957), pp. 13–31.

ideas of liberty and equality, of the rights of men and peoples to participate in determining their own fate and history. They learned of them in missionary schools, in the colleges which the British administration established in India and other colonies, and in the Western institutions of higher learning. Around the turn of the century hundreds of young Indians studied in Cambridge and London; Indo-Chinese and Africans in Paris; Chinese at American universities.

Under the impact of Western ideas a Young Turkish, a Young Indian, a Young Chinese, a Young Arab movement arose in succession to, and under the influence of, the Young Italian, Young Ireland, Young German and Young Russian movements of mid-nineteenth-century Europe. In all these cases the movements were initially confined to small circles of intellectuals and agitators, many of them working and living in exile. They wished to endow their countries with the benefits flowing from the advanced ideas of the age which they had learned from the West. Western books were translated and new literary styles and fashions introduced into the indigenous languages. These small groups acted as a leaven in widening circles; the intellectual agitation was transformed into political action, as soon as outside circumstances favored it. Such an occasion arose when Japan, until recently an isolated backward Oriental kingdom, defeated the Russian empire whose expansion across Asia had been regarded by Britain for almost a century as the greatest threat to itself. This first blow struck by a "colored" people against the apparently irresistible domination of the "white" man left a deep impression on the minds of Asia and Africa. With its slogan Asia for the Asians, Japan became the leader of Young Asia. It had shown that by a disciplined modernization of its national life and structure an Asian people could through its own strength claim and win equality with the great European powers.

Contemporary witnesses have described the impact of the event on Asian and African nationalism. "At the close of the year 1904," C. F. Andrews wrote before World War I, "it was clear to those who were watching the political horizon that great changes were impending in the East. The war between Russia and Japan had kept the surrounding peoples on the tip-toe of expectation. Even the remote villagers talked over the victories of Japan as they sat in their circles and passed round the *huqqa* at night. . . . Asia was moved from one end to the other, and the sleep of the centuries was finally broken. A new chapter was being written in the book of the world's history. Delhi was a meeting-point of Hindus and Musulmans, where their opinions could be noted and recorded. The Musulman, as one expected, regarded the reverses of Russia chiefly from the territorial standpoint. These reversals seemed to mark the limit of the expansion of the Christian nations over the world's surface. The Hindus regarded more the inner significance of the event. The old-time glory and greatness of Asia seemed destined to return. The whole of Buddha-land from Ceylon to Japan might again become one in thought and life. Hinduism might once more bring forth its old treasures of spiritual culture for the benefit of mankind. Behind these dreams and visions was the one exulting hope—that the days of servitude to the West were over and the day of independence had dawned. Much had gone before to prepare the way for such a dawn of hope: the Japanese victories made it, for the first time, shining and radiant."

The same phenomenon was noticed in Africa by an Englishman who had lived there for forty years and who wrote in 1907: "Suddenly and unexpectedly, the conviction that native forces, however brave, were bound to be worsted by Europeans, was shaken to its base by the discovery that Russia, which was regarded in the East as the greatest military Power in Europe, had been driven from pillar to post . . . by a comparatively diminutive and feeble power, whose people, whatever else they might be, were certainly not Caucasians or Christians. It may be said with truth that the native Africans knew nothing about Japan. But yet I should doubt whether there was a town or village in the whole of Africa where the inhabitants did not learn directly or indirectly that the Russian invaders of the Far East had been scattered like sheep by an unknown non-European race." Many years later a perceptive Bengali remembered the impression which the Japanese victory produced on his generation then in its boyhood: "We felt an immense elation, a sort of reassurance in the face of Europeans, and an immense sense of gratitude and hero worship for the Japanese." Dr. Sun Yat-sen stated as late as 1924 that "a new Japan has risen and Japan's success has given the other nations of Asia unlimited hope. . . . Japan's rise has brought prestige not only to the Yamato race, but it has raised the standing of all Asian peoples. We once thought we could not do what the Europeans could do; we see now that Japan has learned from Europe, and that we too will be learning. . . ."[19]

The Japanese victories sparked the Russian Revolution of 1905, a poorly organized uprising without effective leadership. It was directed against autocracy and bureaucratic despotism, against economic backwardness and administrative inefficiency. The Asians were quick to sense similarities in their and the Russian situation. Were not the Asian lands, like Russia, backward agrarian countries with masses living in ignorance and misery, subject to exploitation by the industrially more advanced countries? A wave of revolutionary unrest swept over Asia, not only in colonial lands like India and Egypt, where it was easily contained and partly appeased by efficient government, but above all in the independent nations, ancient theocratic governments like Russia which stood in urgent need of modernization and secularization— Persia, Turkey and China. It is a remarkable fact that whereas the Russians were unable to overthrow autocracy in 1905, the Turks and the Chinese apparently succeeded in 1908 and 1912. Constitutions according to the Western model and greater governmental efficiency in integrating the nation and in caring for the welfare of the masses—these were the demands raised in the leading Asian countries between 1906 and 1914.

The situation was similar in Latin America, where, too, the need for a fundamental modernization of society existed, in order to prevent foreign interference and to raise the level of life of the masses. The outstanding event with which the twentieth century in Latin America opened was the Mexican Revolution of 1910.

[19] Charles F. Andrews, *The Renaissance in India, Its Missionary Aspect* (London: Young People's Missionary Movement), 1912, p. 4. Andrews (1871–1940) lived most of his life in India. Edward Dicey, *The Egypt of the Future* (London: Heinemann, 1907), p. 139 ff. Dicey (1832–1911) was editor of the London *Observer*, 1870–1889, and later settled in Africa. Nirad C. Chaudhuri, *The Autobiography of an Unknown Indian* (New York: Macmillan, 1951), p. 105; Shao Chuan Leng and Norman D. Palmer, *Sun Yat-sen and Communism* (New York: Praeger, 1960), p. 33. See also Lajpat Rai, *The Evolution of Japan and Other Essays* (Calcutta: R. Chatterjee, 1919).

It coincided with the Young Turkish and Young Chinese revolutions and it resulted in the nationalist and socialist program of the Constitution of 1917; under the presidency of General Lázaro Cárdenas the demand of "tierra y libertad," reminiscent of the demand for "zemlya i volya" in the Russia of the 1870's, was realized. This revolution, like those which followed it in Asia and Africa, not only opposed and rejected foreign economic control and political interference, but also emphasized native traditions and values. The resources of the country were to be utilized for the welfare of the people as a whole and the nationalization of vast foreign holdings, a thorough land reform and a rural school movement were put into the service of activating and elevating the illiterate peasant masses. The ancient Aztec cultural heritage was revived. The Mexican Revolution was the first to aim at a nationalist, socialist and cultural reconstruction of all aspects of life. It led to a prolonged and bitter controversy with the United States which was only settled when the latter recognized what it meant for the feeling of dignity of the Mexicans not to have to tolerate in their own country what the United States would not tolerate on its own soil. The same yearning for dignity, the wish to be respected as equal and to be allowed to conduct one's own affairs without interference from abroad, has been the driving motive behind the nationalism in Asia and Africa. As its result the mysterious and unchanging East of the nineteenth century and its hallowed and primitive forms of life have begun to undergo a rapid change. Rarely has so great a contrast been witnessed by history than the one between Asia and Africa in 1905 and today.

The process of decolonization which started in 1905 coincided with the coming to power of the Liberal government in England which on the part of the West assumed the leadership in this incipient process. Speaking at the Liberal meeting in the Albert Hall in London in January 1906 Prime Minister Henry Campbell-Bannerman, a staunch supporter of home rule for Ireland who had opposed and denounced the Boer War, summed up the dominant party view that "militarism, extravagance, protection were weeds which grow in the same field, and if they wanted to clear the field for honest cultivation they must clear them all out. . . . We desire to develop our undeveloped estates in this country—

to colonize our own country. . . . The government was opposed
to aggression and adventure. What nobler role could this great
country assume than at a fitting moment to place itself at the
head of a League of Peace?"

VI

THE FIRST Asian nation in which the events of 1905 evoked a
response of national reform was Persia. Students and merchants
in Teheran forced the Shah in August 1906 to promise to end
court misrule and to introduce constitutional reforms. An English
eyewitness reported his impressions: "The Russian Revolution has
had a most astounding effect here. Events in Russia have been
watched with great attention, and a new spirit would seem to
have come over the people. They are tired of their rulers, and,
taking example from Russia, have come to think that it is possible to have another and better form of government. . . . They
are, of course, absolutely ignorant of the principles of government,
with the exception, perhaps, of a few of their chiefs. When I was
in the Teheran legation, they used to come and ask me how our
constitution was worked, and would show a naïveté which was
almost pathetic. They see clearly the object in view, but they are
very hazy as to the means of attaining it. Undoubtedly it will be
many years before this Parliament can become really effective."
Professor Browne's prognosis proved true. In the more than half
a century which has passed since that time, parliamentary government has as little taken root in Persia as in most other Asian
lands.[20]

In October, 1906 the first Persian parliament, the Mejliss-i-milli,
was opened. Domestic corruption in the cities, tribal rivalry in
the country, and foreign interference prevented its proper functioning. Throughout its often interrupted life, it was unable to
carry through any real reform and to bring Iran nearer to modern
nationhood. Parliamentary "democracy" did not work. Elections
were rigged by the pressures of the court and the big landowners

[20] Edward G. Browne, *The Persian Revolution of 1905-1909* (Cambridge
University Press, 1910), pp. 120 ff. Browne (1862-1902), a British Oriental-
ist, visited Persia first in 1887 and became Adams Professor of Arabic at
Cambridge in 1902.

and often influenced by foreign intrigue. A similar situation existed among most young nations in Asia and Africa but it equally existed in many countries in southern and central-eastern Europe and Latin America. It would be hypocritical to attribute the nonfunctioning of democracy and the establishment of military reform regimes in Afro-Asian nations to the absence of "Caucasian" or "Christian" elements there.

The dissolution of the Iranian Parliament and its replacement by the open dictatorship of the Shah and his premier in May 1961 was apparently well-received by the people. "American visitors have been surprised and shocked to find Iranians rejoicing over the dissolution of Parliament," wrote an American observer. "Sending all the Deputies packing has proved the most popular recent act of the Shah. There is an old Persian saying going the rounds: A seat in the Parliament is costly, but it is more than worth it." Why should American visitors have been so surprised? There was not much regret felt among the French people either over the dissolution of Parliament there in May, 1958 and its replacement by a personal dictatorship.[21]

By its geographic situation Persia was much more remote from contact with Europe than Turkey. Two years after the Persian Revolution of 1906 a similar but in many ways more successful revolution broke out in Turkey. It was not initiated by students and merchants but by a conspiracy of officers. Their demand for a modernization of the medieval theocratic structure of the Ottoman Empire fell on better-prepared ground. The Turkish ruling class like the Russian ruling class had been in touch with Europe since the seventeenth and eighteenth centuries and had introduced, under the pressure of military needs, the first technological borrowings. Augier Ghislain de Busbecq, who from 1556 to 1562 was Ambassador of Emperor Ferdinand I at the court of Suleiman the Magnificent, reported in one of his letters that "no people in the world is more ready to adopt a useful invention than the Turks are. To mention an example, they immediately adopted our small and big guns and other inventions of ours." Jewish and Christian subjects of the Sultan served generally as intermediaries between the technologically advanced West and Turkey. French

[21] Report from *The New York Times* correspondent from Teheran of May 25, 1961.

officers helped to organize in the late eighteenth century military schools for artillery and naval engineering. As in Russia at the time, all reforms, as far as they went—and that was not far—were motivated by purely practical reasons and initiated by the state, not by public demand. Only in the military schools the rudiments of modern science were taught.

A more thorough reform movement was started by the edict of 1839 which established the equality of all subjects irrespective of religion, promised certain legal guarantees for individual rights and the introduction of new codes of law after the European model. The first steps toward Westernizing and secularizing the institutions of the medieval empire were thus taken but they were resisted by the large majority of the Turks. Modern schools opened only after 1857, when the Ministry of Education was established. The most important among them was the Imperial Lycée at Galata (1868), where civil servants were trained and French was used as a language of instruction. A small Turkish intelligentsia came into being; like the similar class in early nineteenth-century Russia, it became from now on the chief driving force for a radical transformation of Turkish society.

At about that time the first pioneering modern man of letters appeared, Ibrahim Sinasi, the son of an army officer, who having studied for five years in France translated, after his return, French poets and founded the first private newspaper. His disciple Namik Kemal started in 1868 the publication of the first free Turkish newspaper in London, Hürriyet (Liberty), about a decade after Alexander Herzen began to publish there the first free Russian periodical. Namik Kemal's patriotic plays and stirring poetry helped to awaken a Turkish national consciousness. The progress of an alert public opinion in the 1870's though limited to a very small circle was not without some significance. In 1859 there had been in all Turkey only one official and one semiofficial weekly; by 1876 there appeared seven Turkish dailies in Constantinople.

Under the pressure of international events, Abdul Hamid, an astute man who became Sultan in that year, promulgated a constitution at the end of 1876; it was short-lived; he soon exiled the advocates of liberal reforms and in 1878 he dissolved the Parliament. A period of thirty years of reactionary despotism now set in. Turkey was jealously guarded against Western or liberal ideas. She was maintained as a medieval Islamic theocracy. No freedom of expression existed. As was the case in Russia under Nicholas I, the men who espoused liberal Westernizing reforms were forced into exile or into conspiracy. The most important among the secret societies was the Ottoman Committee of Union and Progress, the Young Turks as they were frequently called, a group of officers who forced the Sultan in July 1908 to reintroduce the constitution of 1876. For the next ten years Turkey witnessed, under the guise of a constitutional monarchy, the dictatorship of the Young Turks and the rapid awakening of a Turkish nationalism. But the decade was also a period of disaster in the field of foreign policy. The Ottoman Empire was defeated in the war against Italy, in the Balkan War and in the First World War. The Young Turks bore the brunt of these disasters and were unable to carry through radical reforms.

The most prominent personality to lay the foundations of Turkish nationalism in the first quarter of the twentieth century was Ziya Gökalp. He turned from Ottomanism to Turkism, from the community of peoples living under Ottoman rule and in the brotherhood of Islam to the assumed racial and cultural unity of all the populations speaking a Turkish language and looking upon Turan (Turkestan in Central Asia) as their common home. "The feelings pulsing in my blood are the echo of my past," he wrote in one of his poems. "I do not read of the glorious deeds of my ancestors in withered, yellow, dusty pages of history, but in the blood flowing in my veins, in my heart. My Attila, my Genghiz [Khan], heroic figures, are no less of stature than Alexander and Caesar. Still more familiar to my heart is Oguz Khan, an obscure and mysterious figure to historic inquiry. He still lives in my heart and pulses in my veins in all his greatness and glory. Oguz it is that delights my heart, that inspires me to shout exultantly: The Turkish people's fatherland is not Turkey, it is not Turkestan, it is a far-flung land, and eternal: Turan." This semireligious effusion of nationalist sentiment was the typical language of central and eastern European, and soon of Asian and African, nationalism in the twentieth century.

Like all nationalists of the post-liberal period Gökalp glorified the national collectivity over the individual. He approved extreme

nationalism and denied all international obligations. "Since the
nation is the source and model for all [the individual's] ethical
values, morality is for him identical with love of the country and
service to the nation." Like German or Russian romantic nationalists, Gökalp wished to revive the ancient folk traditions and to
"nationalize" religion. He was willing to accept Western technology, but sought the deeper sources for Turkey's cultural revival
in the Turkish past which was glorified and exalted far beyond
historical knowledge. He rejected the Ottoman language, used by
the government and the classical literature, a language composed
of Arabic, Persian and Turkish words and idiomatic phrases, in
favor of the spoken popular Turkish, formerly despised by the
educated class. He believed that its introduction as the literary
language for all Turks would tear down the barriers between the
intellectuals and the masses and thus help to create national
unity. Gökalp's ideas were in a continuous state of development,
for he lived in the "turbulent decade of Turkish history [1908–
1918]" when the modern national movement was born. "Among
the intellectual leaders of this movement Gökalp occupies the
central place."[22]

Gökalp, in order to exalt the Turkish past and to present it as
a source of European civilization, had to take recourse to many
rather daring and imaginative interpretations of history. Nor could
he establish a living fruitful link between a Turkish nationalism
which emphasized the pre-Islamic legendary past, and Islam which
had drawn its chief cultural inspirations from Arabic and Persian
sources. In that respect the national reform movement among
the Arabs, especially in Egypt, could build on more solid foundations in working out a synthesis of tradition and modernism. As
soon as Mustafa Kemal, by his victory over the Greeks, had
acquired the power and the prestige which the Young Turks never
possessed, he threw tradition overboard and decided whole-
heartedly for the full Westernization of Turkey in the name of
nationalism.

For more than a century the Ottoman empire, once so power-

[22] See the excellent monograph by Uriel Heyd, *Foundations of Turkish
Nationalism. The Life and Teachings of Ziya Gökalp* (London: Luzac,
1950) and Zia Gökalp, *Turkish Nationalism and Western Civilization*, tr. by
Niyazi Berkos (London: Allen & Unwin, 1959).

ful, had like the Chinese empire suffered grievous humiliations on the part of the powers, even on the part of its own former subjects. In 1922, however, Turkey under Kemal's leadership inflicted a smashing defeat on its "hereditary enemy," the Greeks. Supported by the British, the Greeks wished to bring their revolt against the Turks which had started one century before to a total and victorious conclusion and to re-establish the great Greek empire of the early Middle Ages. They were driven out of the Turkish homeland and, as a result of this unexpected victory, Turkey became the only one of the five defeated nations of World War I which could repudiate the peace treaty imposed by the victors (and the peace treaty of Sèvres was infinitely more severe than that of Versailles), and replace it by a peace treaty negotiated freely between equals, the treaty of Lausanne which recognized all Turkish national aspirations. Kemal looked with contempt upon Turkey's prenationalist Ottoman and Islamic past which had known so many humiliating defeats and frustrations for the last one hundred and fifty years. Like Gökalp he sought the source of inspiration for a new Turkey in the pre-Islamic, heroic and primitive past, which he identified with a supposed purity of the Turkish national spirit. He went much farther than Gökalp in his desire for a radical Westernization, in turning away from the Asian and Islamic past of Turkey. "Under the [Ottoman] empire," he said in 1923, "the governments of the Sultan did their best to hinder the Turkish nation from a free intercourse with Europe. . . . We nationalists are open-minded people. Definitely our country will be a modern and progressive one." One year later he asked: "Is it possible that a nation which wants to be really civilized can stay outside the West? There are many countries but there is one civilization." And again one year later: "Our goal is to reach the place we deserve in the family of civilized nations of the West."

As Professor Halil Inalcik of Ankara University wrote, Mustafa Kemal's victory was "that of Westernization in its most radically conceived form." The state, which became a republic, was entirely separated from religion; Islam was abolished as a political institution. Education, law and literature were thoroughly secularized and Westernized. The language was divested of all its classical (Arab or Persian) associations and was written in Latin instead of

Arabic characters. Even a Western-type parliamentary democracy was accepted as the fairly distant goal and all imperial ambitions recalling real or legendary past glories—Ottoman, Islamic or Turanian—were discarded. Thus, Turkey, more than Egypt, India or Japan, set an example of a thoroughly Westernized nationalism, cutting the ties with its non-European past.

Kemal's Turkey set a precedent for later developments in its initial cooperation with Soviet Russia and in its establishment of a one-party dictatorship based upon a fervent nationalism and the fascination of a leading personality. At the end of World War I Western imperialism showed in the Sykes-Picot Treaty, the inter-Allied agreement at San Remo and the peace of Sèvres a ruthless disregard of Arab and Turkish national aspirations (and of the democratic principles of Western civilization). The Arabs were at that time neither united nor organized to a degree which would have made resistance possible. The Turks were, thanks to Mustafa Kemal's personality, to their cohesion and to the support of Soviet Russia. Lenin's seizure of power terminated the secret wartime treaties between Russia and her Allies, which had promised, in case of victory, Constantinople and the Straits to Russia, and brought about a reversal of alliances. Turkey's Caucasian rear was now protected by friendship with the Soviet republics; Russian supply of arms made Turkish victories over the Armenians and Greeks possible; on March 16, 1921 the Soviet government and the revolutionary government of Mustafa Kemal concluded a treaty the preamble of which proclaimed: "The two parties to this treaty hereby affirm that, in their struggle for liberation, the peoples of the East are at one with the workers of Russia fighting for a new social order. They emphatically proclaim the right of the peoples of the East to liberty and independence and a form of government in accordance with their own desires."

A close friendship united Turkey and Soviet Russia in the 1920's. Soviet help made it possible for Turkey, in the difficult years between the Treaty of Sèvres and the Treaty of Lausanne to show Europe a bold front: the Soviet Union's renunciation of the Russian capitulations and concessions in Turkey prepared the way for the country's political and economic regeneration; Russia in 1921 even restored the cities and districts of Kars and Ardahan, which she had gained as a result of the war with Turkey in 1878, to the latter. But Communist doctrines were as little allowed to make headway in Kemalist Turkey as later in Nasser's United Arab Republic. Without damaging her friendship with the Soviet Union, Turkey tried to keep open all ways leading to a friendly and cooperative West. At a time when the term was not yet in general use, nationalist Turkey followed a policy of positive neutralism, based upon a sober weighing of its national interest. Therein she acted as all the Western nations of that period did.

Kemal's revolutionary reform regime was, like that of Bourguiba in Tunis or that of Nasser in Egypt, a republican dictatorship of one man leading, and backed by, a well-organized and disciplined party, the Republican People's Party, which held for more than twenty years an absolute monopoly of all political life. Only in 1950 an opposition party was allowed to gain power in free elections. For ten years Turkey had an outwardly democratic parliamentary multi-party regime: in 1960 it was overthrown by the combined efforts of students and officers and at least temporarily the officers' junta ruled the country. At the end of forty years of reform, seventy percent of the population was still illiterate, the economy was shaky, the poverty great. Traditional Islam kept the loyalty of the people in country towns and villages. Yet among the youth Kemalism had taken root. The hope of the birth of a modern nation had not been in vain, though the road ahead was long. Perhaps Mustafa Kemal had demanded too much, had not taken efficient account of continuing traditional cultural needs, had like most men of his generation not sufficiently understood the need of greater social democracy in underdeveloped countries. The coming years will show how far the young Turkish generation has learned the lesson and will be able to transform Turkey into a bridge connecting West and East.

VII

FOUR years after the medieval Ottoman Empire succumbed to the onrush of modern nationalism, the same fate overcame the ancient Chinese empire. The dynasty was overthrown in the Revolution which started in October, 1911 and brought the abdication of the last emperor in February, 1912. In both cases external pressures speeded up a domestic struggle against autocracy, traditionalism and foreign interference. In the first case it was the threat of partition presented by the British–Russian agreement of 1907 and the Allied–Greek attempt at dismembering Turkey after 1918. The Chinese acted under the impact of the growing economic and territorial interference of foreign powers following the Boxer rebellion. In the late nineteenth century Western powers concentrated on the partition of Africa; now they were ready, apparently, to switch to divide up China. In Turkey, according to the structure and traditions of the country, officers assumed the leadership of nationalism; in China this role fell to intellectuals and scholars of whom K'ang Yu-wei, Liang Ch'i-ch'ao and Sun Yat-sen were the most prominent. The progress of nationalism from humanitarian beginnings to political radicalism, typical for European developments, can be followed in China, too. K'ang sought a rational and enlightened reform of Confucianism based on critical learning; he remained until his end (he died in 1927) a constitutional monarchist; he did not glorify national self-sufficiency and firmly believed in world unity and world peace. In his famous Ta-T'ung shu, which he worked out before the Chinese revolution, "he urged the necessity for the abolition of national barriers. . . . He drew the moral [from history] that as civilization advanced in the West so the virus of nationalism became worse and the ability to slaughter more infamous. Therefore the barriers between nations must be broken down and all peoples come under the authority of a World Council composed of representatives of all countries. . . . The attraction of the West [to him] was, in the last resort, that its civilization opened up a vision of a world civilization."[23]

K'ang's disciple Liang, fifteen years younger than his teacher, joined the new republican party: he sided with the Literary Revolution started by Hu Shih in 1917 at the National University in Peking, where Liang applied modern critical methods to the study of Chinese history and accelerated thereby the "revolution in thinking." He went far beyond K'ang in his nationalism. "Education is the means by which a country nurtures its own kind of people," he wrote in 1902, "welding them together as a whole

[23] See E. R. Hughes, The Invasion of China by the Western World (New York: Macmillan, 1938), pp. 113 ff., 152, 163 ff., 128 ff.

that they may be independent and struggle to survive in this world where victory goes to the fit and defeat to the unfit. . . . Those who have a mind to this great business of education, must first recognize the two principles of education, the one the tool for manufacturing the people of the country, the other an indispensable means for understanding the world's experience, for examining the tendencies all over the world and the special characteristics of our own race with a view to arousing its whole strength." Dr. Hu Shih in his autobiography, *Ssu-shih tzu-shuh* (1933), described how eagerly he and his generation in Shanghai admired Liang's articles in *Min Pao* (The People's Newspaper), published in Tokyo in 1902. Their emphasis was on *"Hsin min,"* a new people. His approach had much in common with Nikolai Chernyshevski's in his didactic novel of Young Russia, *What to do? Tales about the New People*.[24] Liang bid China's youth to study Western institutions, but he warned that without a new people the new institutions would not work. Western institutions according to Liang who therein differed from his teacher K'ang, work so well because they are inspired by a virile nationalism which China must acquire. In the West people of the same country and race regard each other as brothers and work above all to be independent and self-governing. Thence they have the power to govern other people, whether by military force, by commerce and industry, or by the church. Nationalism was the secret of Western power; the lack of nationalism, the reason for China's humiliating weakness. The Chinese had been engrossed in family and local loyalties: these had to give way now to *"ai kuo,"* love of country. This new feeling, which found its expression also in the Literary Revolution, had by 1920 become the common attitude of educated youth in colleges and high schools. It was no longer primarily intellectual, but political. The Chinese terms used for "liberty," "equality," "rights," "public opinion," "independence," and "self-government" gained modern Western connotations and were influenced by thinkers like John Dewey and Bertrand Russell. Hu Shih and his friend Ch'en Tu-hsiu who edited the radical periodical *Hsin Ch'ing-nien* (New Youth) recognize that "the strength and brilliance of Europe today . . . comes from the grace of revolution. . . . Revolution means the stripping away of the

24 See Hans Kohn, *The Mind of Modern Russia*, op. cit., pp. 138–154.

old and the change to the new. . . . The history of modern European civilization may well be called a revolutionary history."

Revolution—political, cultural, social—became the dominant issue in twentieth-century China. In its past the Chinese had shown a temperament of reasonableness and nonmilitarism. This changed under the Western impact of nationalism, a nationalism transmitted to the Chinese in the climate of the twentieth century with its two great European wars, its Fascism and Communism. Dr. Hu Shih, perhaps the most Westernized and liberal of China's scholars, spoke of this new spirit in lectures which he delivered in Chicago in 1933: "A Chinese scholar once remarked: 'It is easy for China to acquire the civilization of the West, but it is very difficult to master its barbarism. Yet I suppose we must first master this barbarism, before we can feel at home in this new civilization.' By barbarism he means the military side of the Western culture, which does not consist of mere up-to-date equipment . . . but which must presuppose the existence of what may be vaguely termed 'the martial spirit,' under which term we may include the love for adventure, the almost primitive delight in competitive combat, the instinctive love and worship of the warrior, the painstaking cultivation of bodily strength, the habit of obedience, and the readiness to fight and die for an impersonal cause."[25]

Less than three years after the Chinese Revolution the great European war started. It changed the pro-Western outlook of Sun Yat-sen as it disillusioned many other educated Chinese. The moral prestige of Europe suffered badly, and the new attitude of cynicism towards the West was reinforced by the treatment which China received in Paris (1919) and in Washington (1922). At the same time the student demonstrations in Shanghai on May 4, 1919 and May 30, 1925, revealed the new feeling of self-confidence and the rapid growth of "anti-imperialism," the demand for the immediate termination of the "unequal treaties," the various territorial and economic concessions and juridical and financial privileges imposed by the Western powers and Russia upon China in her prenationalist stage of effete weakness. Soviet Russia's

[25] Hu Shih, *The Chinese Renaissance* (University of Chicago Press, 1933), p. 14.

readiness to accede to these demands, and Western procrastination and refusal, turned the Nationalist Party (Kuomintang) under Sun Yat-sen's leadership to seek help from Soviet Russia. The Chinese nationalist revolution had from the beginning attracted Lenin's attention and sympathy.[26]

After the failure of the Russian Revolution of 1905, when the workers of St. Petersburg and Moscow received no help from their "class comrades" in the West, Lenin despaired of the Western proletariat, especially of its leaders who had "betrayed" socialism. To counter this "decay," Lenin looked hopefully to Asia. At the Bolshevik conference in January, 1912, he welcomed the Chinese revolution, "from our point of view an event of world importance towards achieving the liberation of Asia and the overthrow of European mastery." In an article published for the thirtieth anniversary of the death of Karl Marx (1913) he saw great storms breaking over Asia. "We are now living right in the midst of the epoch of these storms and their reflex action on Europe. Whatever may be the fate of the great Chinese revolution, against which various civilized hyenas are now sharpening their teeth, no forces in the world will restore the old serfdom in Asia or eradicate from the earth the heroic democracy of the popular masses in the Asiatic and semi-Asiatic countries."[27]

In 1921 Lenin's envoy Adolf Joffe offered Russia's help to Sun Yat-sen. This help deeply influenced the course of Chinese recent history in the sense of Communism and totalitarianism. In his *San Min Chu I* (The Three Principles of the People), lectures which Dr. Sun delivered in 1924 and which became the canonized platform of the Kuomintang, he violently attacked Western imperialism. He went so far as to express fears lest China be completely absorbed and her people liquidated by the overwhelming power of the West. He called on China to provide leadership for India and all oppressed peoples toward a new freedom. Whereas formerly Dr. Sun had stressed individual freedom, he now demanded fullest attachment to the totalitarian Kuomintang party and to its unity. "In order that all members [of the party] may be

[26] See Chow Tse-tsung, *The May Fourth Movement* (Harvard University Press, 1960).

[27] Marx, Engels, Lenin and Stalin, *On the Theory of Marxism* (Little Lenin Library, New York: International Publishers, n.d.), p. 24.

united spiritually, the first thing is to sacrifice freedom, then the whole party will have freedom. If the individual can offer his abilities, then the whole party will possess ability." Dr. Sun was not a Communist. In his deep disillusionment with the West he sought Communist help, but the totalitarian principles of Communism and Fascism corresponded to certain authoritarian aspects of Chinese history. "There was thus a swing back to the ingrained tradition of the Chinese family and state, that unity and harmony are the ultimate requisites for which, if necessary, the liberty of the individual must be sacrificed."[28]

Sun Yat-sen did not live to see the triumph of the Nationalist Party. Before his death in March, 1925 he sent a letter to the leaders of the Soviet Union, praising "the heritage left by the immortal Lenin to the oppressed peoples of the world. With the help of that heritage the victims of imperialism will be able to achieve emancipation from that international regime which has been based for ages upon slavery, wars and injustice. I leave behind me a Party which, as I always hoped, will be bound up with you in the historic work of the final liberation of China and other exploited countries from the yoke of imperialism. By the will of fate I must leave my work unfinished and hand it over to those who, remaining faithful to the principles and teachings of the Party, will thereby be my true followers. Therefore I charge the Kuomintang to continue the work of the revolutionary nationalist movement, so that China, reduced by the imperialists to the position of a semicolonial country, shall become free. . . . Taking my leave of you, dear comrades, I want to express the hope that the day will come when the U. S. S. R. will welcome a friend and ally in a mighty free China, and that in the great struggle for the liberation of the oppressed peoples of the world both those allies will go forward to victory hand in hand."

Russian officers, administrators and agitators helped the organization of the Kuomintang to such a degree that under Chiang K'ai-shek the Kuomintang army could establish a National government in Nanking in 1927. Chiang who had received his military training in Moscow, split with the Communists, and from that time on both parties, the Nationalist party of Chiang and the Communist party under Mao Tse-tung, formed Chinese govern-

[28] E. R. Hughes, op. cit., p. 144.

ments and proclaimed themselves the rightful heirs of Sun Yat-sen's Kuomintang. Perhaps it was "the failure of the Nationalists to carry on the revolution and to adhere to the principles and programs outlined by the founder of the Party" which ultimately led to the breakdown of Chiang's regime.[29]

In any case the Kuomintang authoritarian one-party government, suffering from the ravages of the Japanese War and from its own growing senescent overbureaucratization and inefficiency lost all creative initiative and energy and, in the eyes of the Chinese people, the "mandate from Heaven." Whether Mao's Communist party will keep it, none can foresee. Both regimes represent the spirit of revolutionary nationalism inspired by Sun.[30] Both are militant and militaristic, work through secret-police methods, and stress efficiency and preparedness more than individual liberty or free discussion. Chiang himself put a growing value upon traditional Chinese social virtues. Both movements inherited from Sun's later years and his deep disillusionment with the West a bitter anti-imperialism and a deep rooted Chinese imperial pride. Both of them claim imperial control of Tibet and Mongolia, Formosa and Sinkiang as inalienable parts of the Chinese empire and may claim under favorable circumstances other lands once tributary to China. Both, the Kuomintang and the Communists, established some historical continuity with the great T'ai-p'ing rebellion which

[29] See Shao Chuan Leng and Norman D. Palmer, *Sun Yat-sen and Communism* (New York: F. A. Praeger, 1960), p. 180. See there also Sun's interesting remarks on individual liberty and representative democracy, pp. 150 and 188. They are characteristic for much of twentieth-century nationalism.
[30] Liang differed from Sun in his rejection of revolutionary theories. He believed that government interference ran counter to the Chinese character. Revolution was needed in the "materialistic" West with its class oppression. Liang, disillusioned with Western war spirit and imperialism, returned in his last years to a faith in Chinese "spirituality," similar to the attitudes of Slavophiles and others. Hu Shih as a faithful liberal defended modern Western civilization after the First World War: "Today the most baseless and, moreover, the most poisonous legend is the deprecation of Western civilization as 'merely materialistic' and the honoring of Eastern civilization as 'spiritual.' This is fundamentally a very old view, but today it seems to be having a new vogue." See Joseph R. Levenson, *Liang Ch'i-ch'ao and the Mind of Modern China* (Harvard University Press, 1953), p. 214. Liang condemned the West for its materialism, the Chinese Communists condemned it for its capitalism.

held central China under its sway from 1851 to 1865. This protest against a dynasty unable to cope with national humiliation by foreign barbarians and with economic ruin, "was in many respects the pilot which illuminated and lit the flames of modern Chinese revolutions. The T'ai-p'ing leaders were heralded as patriotic revolutionaries by the Nationalists and as forerunners of socialism by the Chinese Communists. When one considers that T'ai-p'ing leaders undertook novel social and economic experiments without foreign ideological help, save for a scanty and perverted knowledge of Christianity, he is not surprised to find the Chinese people later willing to give any kind of revolution a fair trial."[31]

Of the five Asian and African nations which have taken a leading part over the last one hundred years in the awakening of nationalism in the two continents—Egypt, India, Japan, Turkey and China—only the last one has turned to Communism as its form of the national revolution. All five were, in varying ways, influenced by the modern West. They have reacted differently to it, in accordance with their history and their social structure—as have European peoples. For there will always be great diversity in the nascent unity of mankind; in its member societies continuity and sweeping revolutionary changes will enter into a dialectic relationship which will insure the diversity within the universal society of the future. Conditions of the past and circumstances of experience may fashion individuals and societies but there always has been in history, and there will be to a growing degree, room for the freedom of men's decision and the power of personality in meeting the challenges of changing conditions and circumstances. If China has turned to Communism, the reason for it has to be sought not

[31] Paul M. A. Linebarger, Djang C. R. and Ardath W. Burks, *Far Eastern Governments and Politics* (New York: D. Van Nostrand, 1954), p. 103. Professor Linebarger wrote in his *The Political Doctrines of Sun Yat-sen* (Baltimore: Johns Hopkins Press, 1937), p. 203 that Sun's program involved "use of China's resurgence of national power to restore the benevolent hegemony which the Chinese had exercised over Eastern Asia, and possibly to extend it over the whole world." In his famous speech of November 28, 1924, in Kobe, Japan, Dr. Sun advocated a Pan-Asian movement based on the Oriental tradition of the rule of Right as against the Western tradition of the rule of Might. Japan was urged to join with China to lead the oppressed peoples of Asia in their fight for liberation and in the establishment of a civilization of peace for all.

only in the events of the 1940's—the long involvement in war with Japan, the disintegration of economic life, the demoralization of the Kuomintang—but in the preceding decades, in the sharp rejection of Confucian traditionalism as an insufficient spiritual nourishment and in the deep disillusionment with the West. In the West, too, nationalism seemed no longer to carry the message of the Enlightenment, of emancipation, of equality and peace, but of self-assertion, and disregard for the rights and interests of others, introducing a system of double bookkeeping in the ethics of international relations, and wearing the mark of hypocrisy.

The West's own abandonment of the professed principles of modern civilization, the abasement of Christianity into a helpmate of the established authorities, of their nationalism and imperialism, turned the West's friends into doubters and cynics. The war of 1914–18 undermined the prestige of the West; worse still was the fact that the events after 1918 in China as well as in the Middle East seemed to prove that liberty was meant only for the Europeans and for the strong. The Turks and the Japanese were able to prove their strength in the only way which the West seemed to respect, by military efficiency, but in China the "unequal treaties" continued to be maintained by the United States and Great Britain until 1943, to a time more than twenty years later than did Lenin's Russia. These were years which counted heavily in the rapid revolutionary transformation of Chinese thought. During the same years Communist China maintained its own government and army, carried through its reforms and indoctrination, built its dedicated cadres. The bitter memories of 1927 intensified the mutual distrust. Thus unique conditions, unknown anywhere else, existed in China at the end of World War II. Through its long duration, its migrations, inflation and suffering, the war had accelerated the social and intellectual revolution even in the more remote parts of the vast and overpopulated realm. In the midst of the decay of the Kuomintang and the general despair, the Chinese Communists stood ready to take over in conditions existing only in China.

The disenchantment with the West was not confined to China where it assumed its most extreme form. Examples when the West seemed unfaithful to its own principles were many. To name only one, even as dedicated a friend of, and believer in, the West and

in French liberalism as Habib Bourguiba of Tunisia found himself
in 1961 in a situation where he came in conflict with Western
self-centered nationalism and militarism. In July, 1961 the French
army fighting in Bizerte repeated some of the haughty excesses to
which it had accustomed itself in six years of colonial war in Algeria, and General de Gaulle rejected the right of the international
organization where so many weak and "inferior" nations are represented to mediate in cases where such a great power as France
in a majestic disregard of the rights and lives of others had acted.
The weekly *Afrique Action* which reflects Bourguiba's views wrote
then that "never will the European and the Americans understand
how the race of the underdeveloped think and feel. . . . Never
will they consider us as men or nations like themselves. . . . All
cooperation with the West . . . can only be stained with neo-
colonialism. . . . The underdeveloped countries of Africa, Latin
America or Asia . . . will orient their efforts toward and receive
aid from the other underdeveloped countries so as to disengage
themselves progressively [from Western ties]."

In an interview with an American newspaperman Bourguiba declared, on July 28, 1961, "I have never believed the United States
to be colonialist. And if United States solidarity with colonialist
France has prevailed over the principles on which the American
nation is based, then I have been wrong. . . . The results will not
affect us alone but the entire world. If it [the United Nations, with
which France refused to cooperate] cannot settle the affair, then
it has no reason for being. It means that the law of the jungle has
replaced international law and morality." A record of a consistent
cooperation with the West seemed, the Tunisians concluded, to
carry no weight, if any one single Western power was displeased
and wished to teach the underdeveloped country a lesson. The
West even against the better knowledge and against the conscience
of some of its members maintained a unified front against the
underdeveloped country. Western observers reported from Tunis
a widespread feeling that the Western nations denied in the eyes
of the rest of mankind the very principles on the strength of which
they claim to oppose totalitarianism.[32] Thus the nationalist pride
of countries of the North Atlantic Community tended to slow

[32] Dispatches from Tunis in *The Christian Science Monitor*, July 24, 1961,
and in *The New York Times*, July 28 and 29, 1961.

down the difficult and otherwise successful process of accommo-
dation between the West and the underdeveloped countries awakening under the impact of the West.

VIII

THE TRANSFORMATION of society which began around 1905
under the impact of the modern West in Asia, Africa and Latin
America presents a task of immense complexity. It is therefore understandable that it has not been brought near a successful conclusion in the first six decades of the present century. The
transition from pre-modern to modern society has been long and
difficult in Europe, too. The birth of modern Europe was accompanied by much strife and turmoil; even by 1960 the reign of constitutional liberty was not firmly established in a number of
European nations. The devastating events of the present century
—the two great wars and the rise and triumph of totalitarianism—
had their origin in Europe, in the insufficient impact of modern
civilization on European peoples and in their continuing pre-modern traditions. Nor do modern Western ideas fuse easily with the
indigenous traditions of Asia, Africa and Ibero-America. Simultaneous with the influx of the new ideas and forms of life, a new
appreciation of ancient and sometimes forgotten native cultures
was awakened. They were rediscovered and studied by Western
scholars, until the peoples themselves began to see them in a new
light. They drew from them a feeling of pride, a new confidence in
their own strength and potentialities; at the same time the continuing relative backwardness of their country increased the tension
between aspiration and reality. Out of the feeling of weakness on
the one hand, of indignation on the other, a characteristic superiority feeling over modern Western civilization was born which
found expression in Asia as it had formerly in the socially and politically less developed countries of Europe. German romanticists
and militarists loved to glorify the supposed virtues of Germanism
by rejecting the "superficial" and comfort-seeking West; Russian
Slavophiles pitied the materialist West and wished to redeem it;
Indians and other Asians and many Latins looked down, from their
spiritual heights, upon the commercialism of the liberal capitalist
nations, above all the United States. Similarly within the United

States before and during the Civil War, many in the Confederacy claimed to represent a true and aristocratic culture against the dollar-mindedness and the noisy industrialism of the northern Union states.

Yet at the same time German and Russian, Asian and Latin-American nationalists were eager to acquire the know-how, the administrative and technical achievements of the so often despised "capitalistic" or "liberal" West. Their attitude toward the West was ambivalent, as was William II's and Hitler's toward England and Khrushchev's toward the United States: emulation and contempt, respectful attraction and hatred, intermingling in varying degrees. The nationalism of the less developed nations, a fruit of their contact with the West, turned against the West. It discovered and claimed its ancestry in their own past and used this revival and reinterpretation of history to emphasize its unique distinctiveness and to praise its purity from alien influences.

National self-assertiveness has become today a universal phenomenon; it is the outstanding character of the age. Though in an attenuated form, it has become dominant even in modern Western nations like Canada which by 1960 seemed enmeshed in a search for its separate "personality" and showed signs of profound irritation with its powerful and rather uncomprehending neighbor, the United States. The same trend appeared in a more chaotic and contradictory way among the nascent African nations, where the intellectuals are in quest of the *négritude*, a theory proposed by Africans deeply steeped and expressing themselves in French, like Aimé Césaire and Léopold Sédar Senghor.[33] Everywhere nationalism has become cultural and economic as well as political. It stresses not so much individual liberty as group separateness. National independence in all fields, not only political—a new concept

---

[33] The first "modern" French African writer was René Maran, whose novel *Batouala* appeared in 1921 and received the Prix Goncourt. In Maran's pioneer work, which was of greater social than artistic significance, "the exotic was replaced by the human and the European halo was confronted by the challenge of the black man's misery": Mercer Cook in *The New Leader*, Oct. 24, 1960. In 1947 a Senegalese, Alioune Diop, founded a magazine *Présence Africaine* to represent the entire Negro world. Ten years later a Société Africaine de Culture tried to unite all Negro intellectuals on the basis of an assumed cultural racial unity and a desire to break with the dominant Western values in an effort of gaining self-confidence and a sense of identity.

of total group-sovereignty—has become the over-all goal. The mid-twentieth century has witnessed the achievement of national independence to a degree unexpected a century ago, first in central-eastern Europe, then in Asia, finally in Africa.

National independence in itself has solved the essential problems of Asian or African peoples as little as it did those of Italy, Poland or Latin America. The process of nation-building and social modernization of largely premodern societies, whether in Sicily or Portugal, in Burma or Ethiopia, in Bolivia or Guatemala, is by necessity a slow one. Tensions among ethnic and religious groups or among regions with different historical traditions and social structures have continued after independence was achieved. Even individual problems like the imperial frontier of the British Indian empire were not changed by the establishment of the sovereign states of India and Pakistan. On the contrary, the conflict concerning the Pathans in the former Northwest province of British India was intensified when Afghanistan faced Pakistan, and the position of the Himalaya states—Nepal, Bhutan, Sikkim and Kashmir—dividing India from China and Tibet became a more serious aggravation for India than it had been to Britain. After 1945 the problems of the new nations—as those of peoples everywhere—were involved, at least indirectly, in the rapidly developing tension between the West, led by the United States, and the Communist bloc, led by the Soviet Union.

This tension was not always harmful to the development of the new nations. On the contrary, in some ways they profited from it. But it would be wrong to overrate either positively or negatively the influence of Communist propaganda on the process of decolonization. The British proclaimed the independence of Egypt and of India before the "cold war" made itself felt or even was thought of; similarly Ghana became, with British help, independent before Africa was drawn into the cold war competition. Nor did fears of Communism prevent the United States from fulfilling its promise of granting Philippine sovereignty in 1946 or hasten it into doing it. Only in a few unfortunate cases, in which the colonial powers denied the principles of modern civilization, like Indo-China, Algeria or Angola, did Communism, positively or negatively, act as a psychological factor in denying or speeding up independence.

It is in the interest of the West that the movement for human emancipation in Asia, Africa and Latin America, be recognized as a fulfillment of Western, not of Communist aspirations. It plays into the hands of Communism when French officials insist that they keep Algeria in subjection for the sake of the West, or when the Prime Minister of the Union of South Africa declares, in a statement of May 29, 1961, that the newly established South African Republic was a "pillar of Christian Western civilization in Africa" and that he regarded efforts to introduce the principles of liberty and equality as a "manifestation of the grabbing hand of Communism over Africa."[34]

In spite of many aberrations, tolerated to the detriment of the West by Western statesmen and military leaders, modern civilization, having solved the problems of the status of the worker in its industrialized society, was in the sixties of the twentieth century well advanced in solving the problem of the status of under-developed nations in a society which, through the growing impact of nationalism and industrialism, was becoming in all its parts more uniform. The global awakening of the peoples to their rights for equality, dignity and well-being, under the challenge of Western imperialism, has opened the first era of global history and started the first beginnings of a universal intercourse. At the same time nationalism provided a safeguard against growing uniformity and against the establishment of the universal hegemony of any one major power or group of powers. The organization of mankind ahead of us promises to follow the pattern of modern Western civilization—pluralism and diversity.

[34] In 1939, after the German attack on Poland, Josef Weinheber, a Catholic Viennese poet, claimed that National Socialist Germany was the true defender of Christian Western civilization. "Germany must not suffer defeat," he wrote on September 14, 1939 to Korfiz Holm. "Just now I see in Germany *the* Occident, and I wish I could see on the other side one intellectual sharing my attitude (*einen Geistigen von meiner Haltung*)." What strange and arrogant defenders "Western civilization" recently had: South African racialists, German National Socialists, French and Spanish traditionalists.

PART FOUR

THE FIRST ERA OF GLOBAL HISTORY
A UNIVERSAL INTERCOURSE

"One thought ever at the fore—
  That in the Divine Ship, the World
    breasting Time and Space,
  All Peoples of the globe together sail,
    sail the same voyage, are bound to
    the same destination."

                    Walt Whitman, "Old Age Echoes"

"La repartition plus égale des biens et des droits dans ce
monde est le plus grand objet que doivent se proposer ceux
qui mènent les affairs humaines. Je veux seulement que
l'égalité en politique consiste à être également libre."

                    Tocqueville, September 10, 1856

"Demander la liberté pour soi et la refuser aux autres, c'est
la définition du despotisme."

                    Laboulaye, December 4, 1874

I

SINCE the middle of the twentieth century, the age of Pan-Nationalism has presented mankind, above all the West, with the new challenge of the rise of the undeveloped countries, a challenge which overshadows the older challenge of Fascism and Communism. The new world-wide challenge characterizes the first age of global history. Lenin who was born in an underdeveloped country on the border of Asia was one of the first to foresee this development. This foresight accounted for the superiority of his vision over that of Fascism. The latter represented an intensification and convulsion of late European nationalism, not the last stage of capitalism; on the contrary, it was a mighty and overbearing protest against the new age of world-wide intercourse which capitalism has brought about in the spreading framework of modern Western civilization. In spite of his broader vision in this one point, Lenin remained in other respects enmeshed in a typically mid-nineteenth-century Hegelian–Marxian construction of history and in the moral climate of the early twentieth-century era of the cult of violence, which Communism shares with Fascism. Both of these attitudes were intensified by Russian traditional dogmatism and extremism. In the twenty-five years of Stalin's oppressive despotism the traditional forces of Russian or Muscovite parochial nationalism reasserted themselves. The similarity with Fascism, a reassertion of an atavistic parochial nationalism, became more pronounced.

In the growing world community after 1945 Stalinism was an anachronism which doomed Communist Russia to dogmatic sterility and moral primitivity. Khrushchev's effort to regain Lenin's ecumenical vision revitalized Communism. His new emphasis on cooperation with the undeveloped countries, his world-wide travels and the resumption of cultural intercourse with the non-Soviet world changed the style of Soviet diplomacy. At the same time, under the leadership of the United States and Britain, the West became aware of the new revolution in the relationships of mankind which Western ideas and Western imperialism had brought about.

Tocqueville was one of the first to recognize and diagnose this revolution. In the introduction to his *Democracy in America* he wrote: "The gradual development of the principle of equality is, therefore, a providential fact. It has all the chief characteristics of such a fact: it is universal, it is lasting, it constantly eludes all human interference, and all events as well as all men contribute to its program. . . . A new science of politics is needed for a new world. This, however, is what we think of least; placed in the middle of a rapid stream, we obstinately fix our eyes on the ruins that may still be described upon the shore we have left, while the current hurries us away." Tocqueville confined this revolution to the Western or as he called it Christian world. The limitation of vision in this extraordinary man was understandable in the 1830's. Even half a century later the famous German historian Leopold von Ranke who in his old age started to write an (unfinished) "World History" saw mankind from a purely Occidental point of view. His insight into the political and moral forces of history was far below that of Tocqueville.

As a young man—he was thirty-three years old—Ranke published a "History of the Serb Revolution." This pioneer study in the beginnings of Near Eastern nationalism was due to Ranke's acquaintance with the Serb nationalist, Vuk Stefanović Karadžić, who lived in Vienna. Ranke spoke of Serbian "emancipation," of a revolutionary process then starting under Western influence to spread to the underdeveloped countries. But Ranke could not recognize the universality of the historical process, the beginning of which he so well described. Half a century later, in 1879, the old man, then at the zenith of his reputation, published a third edition of his youthful work. Characteristically he shifted the emphasis from revolutionary emancipation to one more appropriate to his conservatism by calling it "Serbia and Turkey in the 19th century." In the concluding remarks he echoed the self-confidence of Bismarck's Europe: "The life of the human kind reposes today in the people of Latin and Germanic descent and those of Slav and even Magyar origin who have joined them and become assimilated to them. In all the diversity of our inner discords, in all the mutual hostility of our trends, we, nevertheless, do form a unit in relationship to the outside world. In other ages, other nations and systems flourished which were animated by different principles, and developed different though in themselves important institutions; at present such nations or systems hardly exist.

Ranke saw the Ottoman Empire overrun and penetrated by Christianity (*das christliche Wesen*). "By Christianity we do not understand exclusively the [Christian] religion; [Christian] culture or civilization would also express only incompletely the meaning of the word. It is the [creative] genius of the Occident. It is the spirit which transforms peoples into orderly armies, which builds roads, digs canals, covers all oceans with fleets and converts them into its property, peoples distant continents with colonies; it is a spirit which has penetrated the depth of nature with exact scholarship, conquered all fields of knowledge and rejuvenated them with ever-new efforts, without losing sight of the eternal truth, which, in spite of all their manifold passions, establishes law and order among men. We see the spiritual force moving ahead in prodigious progress." It is characteristic of the Bismarckian epoch that Ranke's spiritual force of Christianity expressed itself above all in military power, in transforming people into armies, in covering the oceans with navies, and in technological conquest. Ranke saw this "spirit" triumphantly conquering America, Africa, Asia, even China. "In an unflagging advance," the ardent lyrical praise of the pious Christian and venerated father of German historiography concluded, "in many forms, unapproachable, it (the Occident), irresistibly equipped with arms (!) and science, gains the mastery of the world (*bemeistert sich der Welt*)." Of the spirit of emancipation, equality and democracy, which Tocqueville saw irresistibly advancing in the 1830's, the great German historian half a century later noticed nothing. His "spirit" of the Occident or of Christianity carried no hopeful message to the backward or subject peoples.

Tocqueville was less optimistic than Ranke about the future of the "Latin and Germanic" peoples of Europe. In a famous passage at the end of the final volume of his *Democracy in America* he foresaw in the 1830's the world situation which came into being in the 1940's: "There are at the present time," he wrote, "two great nations in the world which started from different points, but seem to tend toward the same end. I allude to the Russians and the Americans. . . . All other nations . . . have stopped or continue to advance with extreme difficulty; these two alone are proceeding with ease and celerity along a path to which no limit can be perceived. . . . The Anglo-American relies upon personal interest to accomplish his ends, and gives free scope to the unguided strength and common sense of the people; the Russian centers all the authority of society in a single arm. The principal instrument of the former is freedom; of the latter, servitude. Their starting point is different, and their causes are not the same; yet each of them seems marked out by the will of heaven to sway the destinies of half the globe."[1]

When in 1945 American and Russian armies met on the Elbe river, in the heart of Germany and in the middle of Europe—an unexpected encounter, not desired by either and brought about by the hubris of Germany's war against modern Western civilization—Tocqueville's prophecy seemed fulfilled. The European nations were for the moment prostrate or deeply wounded; the United States and Russia—the one free, the other authoritarian—emerged as the lonely superpowers in a bipolar world, each of them apparently marked out to sway the destinies of half the globe. This situation was vaguely foreshadowed at the end of World War I; this brief adumbration of coming developments stressed the similarity and the continuity of the two great wars, which terminated an era of history, the era of the European state-system, which Ranke glorified and the transitoriness of which Tocqueville recognized. In 1918, too, for a fleeting moment, mankind, shocked by the war's barbarity, and Europe, physically and morally exhausted by its exactions, hopefully listened to two voices speaking from Washington and Moscow promising to end the slaughter of nations and the inhumanity of the existing order. One of the voices was Lenin's, speaking of peace, national self-determination and social justice. The other was Woodrow Wilson's.

Wilson's role as a prophet of the new age did not come un-

---

[1] For other examples of the foresight of the future role of the United States and of Russia, of the possible conflict between them, and North America's leadership in an alliance with Britain and Western Europe, see Hans Kohn, *American Nationalism, op. cit.*, pp. 32 ff., 195 ff., 77 ff., and *passim.*

expected. Almost twenty years before, in the first year of the twentieth century, Wilson wrote in an article on democracy in *The Atlantic Monthly* of "a new era [that] has come upon us like a sudden vision of things unprophesied. . . . The affairs of the world stand in such a case, the principles for which we have battled the long decades through are now put in such jeopardy amidst the contests of nations, the future of mankind faces so great a peril of reactionary revolution, that our own private business must take its chances along with the greater business of the world at large. We dare not stand neutral." Wilson believed that the cause of individual liberty was at stake, and that America, its champion, would not be able to uphold it for long if the world were permitted to lose faith in the cause; for the United States was its chief defender and had been schooled like no other nation in practical proficiency and self-confidence. "It is only just now that we have awakened to our real relationship to the rest of mankind. Absorbed in our own development, we had fallen into a singular ignorance of the rest of the world . . . we have acquired a false self-confidence, a false self-sufficiency, because we have heeded no successes or failures but our own."

The twentieth century, Wilson believed, would force the Americans out of their isolation. "The East is to be opened and transformed whether we will or no; the standards of the West are to be imposed upon it; nations and peoples which had stood still the centuries through are to be quickened, and made part of the universal world of commerce and of ideas which has so steadily been a-making by the advance of European power from age to age. It is our peculiar duty, as it is also England's, to moderate the process in the interests of liberty; to impart to the peoples thus driven out upon the road of change . . . the habit of law . . . which we long ago got out of the strenuous processes of English history; secure for them, when we may, the free intercourse and the natural development which shall make them at last equal members of the family of nations." Sixteen years later, in his Second Inaugural Address, Wilson declared, "The greatest things that remain to be done must be done with the whole world for stage and in co-operation with the wide and universal forces of mankind. . . . We are provincials no longer. The tragic events of the thirty months of vital turmoil through which we have just passed have made us citizens of the world. There can be no turning back." Like Lenin, and before Lenin, Wilson had outgrown the Europe-centered outlook of the nineteenth century.

In 1919 the bipolarization of the globe between Washington and Moscow, which became manifest in the late 1940's, announced itself. Wilson and Lenin started, as Tocqueville had written, from opposite points and principles. Wilson's call stemmed from the liberal tradition of the modern West: with him the United States assumed, for a short moment, the leadership for which geography and history had prepared it. Lenin's call came at the very moment when, under his leadership, Russia turned away from its growing fruitful contact with the West during the St. Petersburg period of Russian history. Lenin tried to rally Asia and Germany for the struggle against the democracies which had won the war only to lose, by their self-centered nationalism, the fruit of their hard-won victory.

Again the attitudes of the United States and of Soviet Russia after 1919 were similar yet motivated by opposite principles and directed toward opposite ends. Both withdrew into isolationism; the Americans voluntarily, the Russians forced by their temporary weakness and exhaustion. The Russian leadership expected that after careful preparation a favorable moment for assuming leadership would sooner or later arrive (and German aggressiveness provided the occasion in 1939 and 1941); the American people hoped that the day of United States leadership would never come (and their hopes were frustrated by Japanese, German and Russian aggressiveness). In the late 1940's, however, the situation foreseen by Tocqueville was accepted as a lasting reality. The Russians were convinced that they were called upon by history to make the world safe for Communism and that global Communist victory was assured; some Americans thought or spoke of an American century and believed that they had to make the world safe for democracy. These expectations proved illusions: by 1960 the brief interlude of the bipolarization of the globe was fading and mankind reasserted itself in its complexity and diversity. The survival of mankind in its nascent unity was only possible on a pluralistic basis, in mutual tolerance and forbearance—that means in the tradition of the modern West.

II

THIS nascent unity was anticipated, though most imperfectly, in the formation of the League of Nations. In the Fall of 1916 the British Foreign Office submitted a memorandum to the Prime Minister which proposed with a sober realism the creation of a league of nations: "We are under no illusion that such an instrument will become really effective until nations have learned to subordinate their personal and individual ambitions and dreams for the benefit of the community of nations. . . . If America could be persuaded to associate itself to such a league of nations, a weight and influence might be secured for its decisions that would materially promote the objects for which it had been created."America expressed its willingness to participate a year later in Woodrow Wilson's "fourteenth point," which demanded the formation of "a general association of nations under specific covenants for the purpose of affording mutual guarantees of political independence and territorial integrity to great and small nations alike."

This association was further defined in Wilson's "Four Ends" speech of July 4, 1918, in which he put forward as one of the ends "the establishment of an organization of peace which shall make it certain that the combined power of free nations will check every invasion of right and serve to make peace and justice the more secure by affording a definite tribunal of opinion to which all must submit and by which every international readjustment that cannot be amicably agreed upon by the peoples directly concerned shall be sanctioned. These great objects can be put into a single sentence: What we seek is the reign of law, based upon the consent of the governed and sustained by the organized opinion of mankind."

In connection with the League of Nations three other principles were affirmed, one which was the legacy of the nineteenth century, two others which opened new vistas. The first one was covered in the "Four Principles" speech of February 11, 1918, in which Wilson declared that "every territorial settlement must be made in the interest and for the benefit of the populations concerned, all well-defined national aspirations shall be accorded the utmost satisfaction that can be accorded them without introducing new or perpetuating old elements of discord and antagonism that would be likely in time to break the peace of Europe, and consequently of the world." Though Europe remained in the center, Wilson's vision, embodied at least partly in the peace treaties, rose to include submerged continents, peoples and classes. Point five of the Fourteen Points demanded that in all colonial questions "the interests of the [colonial] populations must have equal weight" with those of the colonial governments. Accordingly, the peace treaty of Versailles contained a new and promising departure in international law by establishing, at least for the territories ceded by Germany and Turkey, a trusteeship of administrative powers over "underdeveloped" people under the supervision of the League of Nations. The administrators officially assumed obligations both toward the population of the mandated territories and toward the League of Nations. The practice, of course, fell far short of the intentions. The mandates over former Turkish territories were imposed against the will of the populations, those over the former German colonies in Africa did not even envisage the future self-determination of the people. There was a nascent Arab national movement, stimulated during the war by Allied propaganda and promises; the possibility of African national movements was then hardly envisaged by anyone. But at least a beginning was made in the recognition of the principle "that a colonial power acts not as an owner of its colonies but as trustee for the natives and for the interests of the society of nations" and "that the terms on which the colonial administration is constructed are a matter of international concern and may legitimately be the subject of international concern."[2]

The peace treaties of Paris in 1919 offered another far-reaching innovation in establishing the protection of the moral and material rights of labor in all countries by international regulation and supervision. In the supervising body, the International Labor Organization, employers and workers were to be represented on a footing of equality. The Organization, to quote its first director, the French Socialist Albert Thomas, "has helped to popularize among the individual masses, both of the workers and even of the

[2] In the official commentary to the "Fourteen Points" written by F. Cobb and Walter Lippmann. *Foreign Relations of the United States,* 1918, I, 405 ff.

employers, the idea of peace based on an economic understanding and the social solidarity of the nations." These steps—the League of Nations, the trusteeship principle in the administration of dependencies, the international organization to secure humane conditions and social justice "for all peoples everywhere"—marked a milestone on the road to a world order. But little came of it in the immediate postwar period. The growing intensity of nationalism and imperialism everywhere destroyed the promising beginnings and prepared the crises which brought about World War II. Modern Western civilization never seemed so weak by inward decay and so doomed by outward hostility as in the 1930's. It has always been easier for men to sacrifice their lives and even their fortunes than to abandon their habitual ways of thought and feeling, their prejudices and traditions. To think and feel "nationally" had been ingrained in man's mind by the end of the nineteenth century; it demanded great wisdom and courage to see that after World War I nationalism was not enough. The Europe-centered view of the nineteenth century dominated the League which became an instrument of the often conflicting policies of France and Great Britain. After 1919 modern Western civilization, instead of learning the lessons of the war and boldly vitalizing new means for the equality of men and an international order, frivolously and comfortably denied its own principles.

III

THESE principles and their underlying philosophy were not new. Immanuel Kant defined them at the end of the eighteenth century. This greatest philosopher of the Enlightenment lived his whole life in Königsberg, a small city on the eastern fringe of Prussia, outside Germany, on all sides surrounded by Polish territory and later close to Russia's new border. From this far away outpost, which he never left during his long life, Kant enthusiastically welcomed the French Revolution and continued to admire it long after many of its early friends had turned away from its excesses. His outlook could be summed up in a demand for individual liberty and autonomy; his vision embraced mankind as a universal unity of free individuals and equal peoples. He saw modern civilization as the progress from subjugation to self-rule, from dogmatic slumber to critical reasoning. He knew that it was a young civilization. "It is only in the last hundred years," he wrote in his *Reflections*, "that we have opened up communication with the other continents beyond the Seas. America. Japan. The South Sea Islands. It is only in the last hundred years that we have the system of constitutional rule of one great country; England. As regards international law, we are barbarians even now. We have no general educational system yet. A new age." In these words Kant expressed the conviction that his century marked the beginning of a new period of mankind: for the first time the whole globe was being opened up; for the first time the foundations of progressive constitutional government had been laid and England was leading mankind, Western civilization first, the other continents later, on the road to liberty; yet, as regards international law, no definite first step had yet been taken and no system for the education of humanity had been developed. The only real contribution which a nation can make to human living, Kant taught, was to help the progress of all towards a universal order of liberty and law. He found bitter words to condemn all forms of colonialism and exploitation.[3]

Kant's essay "On Perpetual Peace" (1798) was not a utopian dream based upon an optimistic evaluation of human nature. It did not foresee a world government or a world union of states. Kant was afraid that such a "universal order" might usher in a universal despotism. He clearly recognized the beneficial diversity of mankind and of human institutions. He was aware of the antisocial impulses of man (*Ungeselligkeit*), the urge for lawlessness, which has been controlled within national societies by governments and constitutions, especially in states where power is exercised according to well-defined laws made with the consent of the citizens. But the control of man's antisocial impulses is always in danger of breaking down on account of the "barbaric freedom" with which states behave in international relations.

Today there is much talk of the horrors of nuclear warfare as a deterrent of war. Long before the introduction of the modern destructive weapons Kant foresaw that the need for leading a civilized life will force men into establishing an international order

[3] See Hans Kohn, *The Idea of Nationalism, op. cit.*, pp. 395–402, 694–697, and Carl J. Friedrich, *Inevitable Peace* (Harvard University Press, 1948).

of law. The present system of "barbaric freedom" will, "by causing the dedication of all national energies and resources to war, by the desolation of war and still more by causing the necessity of standing continually in a state of preparation for war," force the states to introduce a cosmopolitan condition of security (*einen weltbürgerlichen Zustand der öffentlichen Staatssicherheit*). Then the good and constructive impulses of human nature may become capable of full development. Today, the wickedness of man, contained within each civilized state by the compulsion of law, becomes unmistakably apparent in the relationship of states with each other. Only an international order will be able to contain the lawless inclinations of the human kind and allow the secure growth of man's moral predisposition.

The realistic caution with which Kant approached the problem of perpetual peace was summed up in the last words of his essay: "If it is a duty, and if at the same time there is well-founded hope, that we make real a state of public law, even if only in an infinitely gradual approximation, then the perpetual peace which will replace the peace-makings, falsely so called because they are really only armistices, is no empty idea, but a task which, solved step by step, steadily approaches its goal, since it can be hoped that the periods within which equal progress is achieved will become shorter and shorter." Like Benjamin Constant, Kant regarded the commercial spirit (*Handelsgeist*) as one of the chief factors promoting peace in modern times: "It is the spirit of commerce which cannot coexist with war. Sooner or later it will take hold of every nation. With the money power being perhaps the most reliable among all the powers subordinated to the state power, the states will find themselves impelled (though hardly by moral compulsion) to promote the noble peace and to try to avert war by mediation whenever war threatens to break out anywhere in the world."

Kant's common sense expressed itself in warnings which are even more valid today than they were in his own time: "No state at war with another shall permit such acts of warfare as must make mutual confidence impossible in time of future peace, such as the employment of assassins, of poisoners . . . the instigation of treason in the state against which it is making war, etc. These are dishonorable stratagems. Some sort of confidence in the enemy's frame of mind must remain even in the midst of war, because otherwise no peace could be concluded, and the conflict would degenerate into a war of extermination. For after all, war is only the regrettable instrument of asserting one's right by force in the primitive state of nature (where there exists no court to decide in accordance with law). . . . A war of extermination . . . would allow perpetual peace only upon the graveyard of the whole human race. Such a war therefore, as well as the use of the means which might be employed in it, is wholly forbidden. . . . That such methods of war inevitably lead to such a result is clear from the fact that such hellish arts, because they are in themselves degrading, when once used, do not continue long within the limits of war but are continued in time of peace and thus completely frustrate the purpose of peace."

"Proud of its independence, each nation will rather employ the barbaric means of war, by which that which is being sought, namely the right of each state, cannot be found," Kant wrote. He demanded that at the end of a war the people should call a day of atonement and pray to heaven for forgiveness for having refused to adapt itself to a legal constitution in its relation to other nations. "The celebrations of victory in war and the hymns which (in good Old Testament style) are sung to the Lord of Hosts, contrast equally sharply with the moral idea of the father of mankind; because the people, besides the indifference concerning the manner in which they seek their mutual right (which is lamentable enough), rejoice over having destroyed many people or robbed them of their happiness."

Kant hoped that all nations would accept what he called "a republican constitution," meaning by that the example of England, a constitution based upon the separation of legislative and executive power and the independence of the judiciary. Only representative governments, he thought, are capable of observing the three fundamental principles of true government—"first, the principle of freedom of all members of a society as men; second, the principle of the dependence of all upon a single common legislation as subjects; and third, the principle of the equality of all as citizens. . . . Republicanism means the constitutional principle according to which the executive power is separated from the legislative power. . . . For all forms of government which are not representative are essentially without form, because the legislator cannot be at the same time the executor of the legislative will."

Besides proclaiming the principles of nineteenth-century democracy, Kant anticipated the needs of the twentieth century. "The narrower or wider community of all nations on earth," he wrote, "has in fact progressed so far that a violation of law and right in one place is felt in all others. Hence the idea of a cosmopolitan or world law is not a fantastic and utopian way of looking at law, but a necessary completion of the unwritten code of constitutional and international law to make it a public law of mankind." Kant wrote as a common sense observer of international behavior and as one of the first to grasp the global unity of history based upon the equality of men and the intercourse of all nations. In his "Die Metaphysik der Sitten" (1798) he defined freedom as "independence from the arbitrary compulsion of another," and declared it "the inalienable right of each human being by virtue of his humanity, in so far as such freedom can coexist with the freedom of all other human beings according to universal law." But this freedom can be securely realized only in a "universal civil society founded on law and justice." To establish such a society, he taught in his "Idea of a Universal History in a Cosmopolitan Intent" (1784), was the supreme task for the human species. In a later writing "On the Common Saying that Something may be Right in Theory but not Suitable for Practical Life" (1793) Kant summed up his "practical" reasons for mankind accepting perpetual peace, not so much out of morality as out of necessity:

"The fact that something has not yet succeeded is no proof that it will never succeed; such an argument would not even justify the abandonment of any practical or technical efforts, such as, for example, the attempts to make pleasure excursions in aerostatic balloons. Still less would such a condition justify the abandonment of a moral purpose which, as such, becomes a duty if its realization is not demonstrated to be impossible. Besides all this, many proofs can be given that the human race as a whole is actually further advanced in our age towards what is morally better than it ever was before, and is even considerably so when its present condition is compared with what it has been in all former ages, notwithstanding temporary retrogressions, which, being transitory, can prove nothing against the general position. Hence the cry about the continually increasing degeneracy of the human race arises from the very fact that as it today stands on a higher stage of morality . . . its judgment on what men are in comparison with what they ought to be, becomes—as in our own self-examination—the more severe the more stages of morality mankind has surmounted" in history.

"Universal violence and the evils arising from it at last force a people to subject themselves to the constraint of public law . . . and thus to enter into a civil and political constitution. In like manner, the evils arising from constant wars by which the states seek to reduce or subdue each other, bring them at last, even against their will, to enter into a universal or cosmopolitical constitution. Should such a condition of universal peace [the formation of a world state] prove, by introducing the most terrible despotism, to be more dangerous to liberty than war, then the evils from which deliverance is sought will compel the introduction of a condition among the nations which does not assume the form of a universal commonwealth but of an association regulated by law, according to the right of nations as concerted in common."

Since Kant wrote these lines, the establishment of an association of nations regulated by law and concerting in common, has gained in urgency. It has found its expression in the League of Nations after World War I and in the United Nations after World War II. Both organizations represent the application of the principles of modern Western civilization to the field of international relations. They are also the outcome of the pacifist movement which throughout the nineteenth century was growing in the West. Its organized form began in 1815 in the United States, and London saw the following year the establishment of the British Society for the Promotion of Permanent and Universal Peace. In 1843 the first international pacifist convention was held in London; Elihu Burritt, the learned blacksmith from Connecticut, Richard Cobden and John Bright founded a League of Universal Brotherhood in London, and a corresponding Société d'Union des Peuples was formed in Paris. An international peace congress met in 1848 in Brussels and the American poet John Greenleaf Whittier greeted it in a poem with characteristic utopian hopes:

Evil shall cease and Violence pass away,

*And the tired world breathe free through a long Sabbath
day.*

Almost one year later, in August 1849, a peace congress met in Paris
with Victor Hugo in the chair and Cobden at his side. Tocqueville, then French Foreign Minister, greeted the Congress. Victor Hugo pointed to the example of the French provinces which
after fighting for some centuries had then replaced the sword
by the ballot box; he predicted that the nations of Europe would
similarly fuse in a higher unit while preserving their distinct in-
dividualities. "A day will come," he proclaimed, "when we shall
see these two immense agglomerations, the United States of America and the United States of Europe, facing each other and stretching out the hands across the seas in close cooperation." This, Hugo
was convinced, would happen soon, because railroads and technical
innovations accelerated all developments. But the ballot box lost
its importance on the European continent and the sword regained it with the coming of Napoleon III and Bismarck. In
1850, 1851 and 1853 further peace conferences met in the St.
Paul's church in Frankfurt am Main, in London and Edinburgh.
Then the movement suffered a marked decline.

A decade later the peace movement was resumed, directed now
toward a humanitarian effort to limit the barbarity of war. In 1863
upon the suggestion of Henri Dunant the International Committee of the Red Cross was founded in Geneva and the following year twenty-six governments signed a convention there which
has since been amended and amplified, has been accepted by almost all governments, and has grown into a universal law limiting
the conduct of hostilities. Three years later a Congress for Peace
and Liberty met in Geneva. The organization committee was
headed by Jules Barni, professor at the Academy in Geneva and
translator of Kant. The Congress was dominated by the rhetoric
of Giuseppe Garibaldi, who demanded national self-determination
and the brotherhood of democratic peoples, freed from oppressive
priests and monarchs, as the basis of peace. After the Congress, the
International League for Peace and Liberty was founded which
published as its official newspaper *Les Etats-Unis d'Europe* in
French and in German. The League held various conferences,
most of them in Geneva, all of them in Switzerland. The Franco-

German war of 1870 gave a new impetus to the movement. Many national peace societies were founded and a growing emphasis was put on international arbitration and the development of international law. From 1889 on, regularly every year, Peace Congresses met, the first in Paris on the occasion of the centenary of the French Revolution. It was followed in the same month by the first interparliamentary conference, as a result of which the Inter-Parliamentary Union was organized in 1892, to discuss the most practical means of establishing world peace by simultaneous concerted action within the parliaments of all countries. In 1892 an International Peace Bureau in Berne was founded to coordinate the activities of all peace organizations.

Meanwhile organized international contacts and congresses, hardly known before the middle of the nineteenth century, have grown rapidly in numbers and purpose, until they are covering today every imaginable field of activities and, while formerly confined to Europe, have become world-wide. According to the Union des Associations Internationales twenty international congresses of all kinds met in 1867; 187 in 1910; 455 in 1935; and 1,432 in 1958. "Notre monde qui a rétréci les distances," writes the Bulletin *Associations Internationales*, 1959, No. 6, "s'est en même temps considérablement étendu par l'éveil d'Etats et de continents autrefois dans l'ombre. Concentrée d'abord en quelques villes [d'Europe], l'activité internationale s'est aujourd'hui largement déployée." While distances have been shrinking rapidly these last one hundred years, the horizons of all activities have been immensely broadened at the same time. In 1958 the International Congresses met, besides the United States and Canada, in 26 European, 20 African, 17 Latin American, 15 Asian and 4 Australasian countries. Since that year the number of meetings in Africa and Asia has continued to increase. In these international conferences for the first time representatives of all peoples are meeting and communicating with each other, so that mankind as a whole is represented, an event which changes the meaning of international relations. It marks the birth of pan-humanism, it realizes an all inclusive mankind-concept, and this happens simultaneously with the triumph of the principle of nationalism, the age of pan-nationalism. The United Nations is the outward expression and symbol of the new age.

IV

THE CHARTER of the United Nations crystallized modern Western thought stemming from Bentham, Kant, Mill and Wilson, not from Marx or Lenin. The underlying concepts of war and peace, of the rule of law irrespective of class or caste, of due process of law, of peaceful change, of open debate and of the right to opposition, of parliamentary representation and procedure are irreconcilable with the theory and praxis of premodern or totalitarian societies. For representatives of such societies, the United Nations provides a unique training ground in democratic methods of discussion, methods developed in the long tradition of the British parliament, in the restraint imposed by them, in the necessity to listen to contradiction and to argue in reasonable terms. Elections, discussions and votes are public and subject to the scrutiny of public opinion.

The name of the new world organization was suggested by the name of the United States. It was probably used first in that sense in an article by an American, Hamilton Holt, who wrote in 1910: "The United States furnishes the model for the united nations. The Declaration of Independence foreshadows the declaration of interdependence." Under the impact of the Fascist threat to civilized mankind the concept of unity began to gain wider acceptance. Characteristic for it was the joint resolution, which the House of Representatives and the Senate of the State of North Carolina adopted in March, 1941. "The cornerstone of [Fascist] totalitarianism is the ethnographic state," the resolution read, "whose restricted interests define the scope of its favors; the foundation of democracy is man whose integrity is inviolable and whose welfare is its primary concern. . . . Man must now either consolidate his [fundamental] rights or lose them for generations to come. . . . Just as feudalism served its purpose in human history and was superseded by nationalism, so has nationalism reached its apogee in this generation and yielded its hegemony in the body politic to internationalism. . . . There is no alternative to the [organization] of all nations except endless war."[4]

[4] See the full text of Holt's article and of the joint resolution in *International Conciliation*, no. 342, Sept. 1938, p. 326, and no. 371, June 1941.

At the end of 1941, after the entrance of the United States into the war and at a time of obvious German and Japanese military superiority, I wrote in a book, published early in 1942: "The needs of survival force men into new ways. Only United Nations, developing a growing sense of unity, can win the war. . . . Without the rule of law there can be no disarmament nor peace. No nation can disarm in a lawless world. But law is only law if it is enforced; peace is durable only when backed by the necessary force. . . . Force used for the enforcement of law is necessary to the protection of civilized society against the inroads of barbarism. Even within a peaceful world no panacea for social and economic ills will be found. There are no short cuts to perfection, only the painful and gradual but relentless and tenacious march forward to greater plenty more equally shared by all. This task is there at all times, not only in this crisis [1941–42]. The promise held out in this crisis is not economic benefits but a lawful order within which the freedom and dignity of man can develop. Yet the world-wide order will facilitate the solution of the economic and social problems of modern interdependent industrial and agrarian society. . . . Every tendency towards separation, segregation and exclusiveness, whether based on historical 'rights' or biological 'laws' of nature, undermines the hopes for the defeat of the Fascist challenge and for a peaceful order at the very time when the growth of interdependence and mutuality is ready to mature the seed of the future . . . in a new democracy of man, conscious of his limitations and of the reality of evil; in a new nationalism, de-demonized and de-politized, resting upon free association and liberated from the dead weight of the past; and in a new [global consciousness] which will take up, under the changed conditions of modern technology and with the experience of the ages, the old and ever-new promise of a world order based upon a community of law."[5]

Twenty years later these expectations were not realized. "There are no short cuts to perfection." Nevertheless, the United Nations represents a great progress over the League of Nations. In 1936, sixteen years after its foundation, the League of Nations was moribund; it was deserted by many members, shunned by non-members; it was not backed by the policy of its intellectual sponsors,

[5] Hans Kohn, *World Order in Historical Perspective* (Harvard University Press, 1942), pp. 280–283.

Britain and the United States; it was parochial and not universal; the faith in democracy withered in an air of isolationism and economic depression; Fascism was rapidly gaining in prestige, power and arrogance, and Soviet Russia offered the spectacle of a ghastly terror. Sixteen years after its foundation, the United Nations, in spite of the incredible difficulties involved in its name and purpose in an age of pan-nationalism, is growing in strength. It draws its strength from paying, as Thomas Jefferson would have put it, "a decent respect to the opinion of mankind." The United Nations offers no panacea for the world's ills (there is none) and suffers from all the imperfections of human institutions. Its meetings are full of bitter tensions, but so are those of many national parliaments. Many problems and questions remain unresolved or are settled by compromises unsatisfactory to some sides, but so it is in democracies; only dictators can "solve" problems in the way in which Alexander "untied" the Gordian knot, and some "solutions" are worse than the situation which they "solved." In view of the gravity and complexity of the problems besetting mankind in this period of global expansion and rapid transformation, the United Nations has been, on the whole, successful. It has ceased to be parochial and has become universal or pan-human.

V

THE UNITED NATIONS has been strengthend by the fact that the global structure which Tocqueville foresaw in 1831 and which existed in the late 1940's—the bipolarization into two great power blocs—is disappearing in the 1960's. A bipolarization easily turns the international body into the stage for a duel between the two superpowers competing for the leadership of mankind. The primitive philosophy of "We or They" threatens to capture many minds. It implies that international life is in a state of perpetual crisis, which demands perpetual preparedness in a competition for survival. The leading National Socialist political scientist, Carl Schmitt, based his concept of politics on such an "inescapable" and fundamental (existentialist) antagonism between friend and foe. According to him, this friend-foe relationship dominates all aspects of life. His brilliantly formulated theory deeply influenced

German political thought. It corresponds to the supposed primitive combative instinct of man and above all of this superior "individuality" or "organism," the real hero of history, the state or nation which regards anyone who stands in the way of the realization of one's aspirations as a foe who has to be done away with. This "We or They," "friend or foe" is the underlying common philosophy of Fascism and Communism. It is surcharged with the emotions of a righteous ideology and of a struggle for national survival. "The culminating points of great politics," Schmitt wrote, "are the moments in which the enemy is visualized in concrete clarity as the enemy. . . . War is the result of enmity, for enmity is the existential negation of the existence of another." In the late 1940's Soviet Russia regarded the United States as such an enemy and some in the United States responded in the same way. Democratic and civilized statesmanship, however, knows no such existential, either-or enmity; it will make efforts to mitigate enmity, regarding settlement of disputes and not total victory as a culminating point of politics; it will try, by patient negotiations, to arrive at some, albeit temporary compromise. The United Nations by its nature upholds the democratic and not the totalitarian approach.

The transition from bipolarization in the United Nations to a more pluralistic, complex and hopeful situation was brought about by the growing emancipation and strength of the underdeveloped and colonial countries. In the 1950's the Soviet Union and the United States regarded each fellow nation as either "friend" or "foe," i.e. they demanded uncritical acceptance of the policy of Moscow or Washington. The importance of the existence of "neutral" or "non-committed" nations for the continuation of a free world was not recognized. For a short while it seemed as if the great democracy had accepted the preposterous claim of Communist theory that mankind was divided into two hostile camps, one of them full of all virtue and goodness and the other the very opposite, and that "all events in world politics were inevitably grouped around this single central point." Since 1917 Communists have proclaimed their faith that these two camps are locked in an apocalyptic life-and-death struggle, from which the forces of "good" would inevitably emerge as the victors over the demons of wickedness and transform all human society. This faith, like any Seven Day Adventist expectation, filled many Communist hearts with apparently unshakable confidence and dedication and built, with the help of dogmatism, inquisition and terror, a monolithic cohesion. Some writers in the West, in a bizarre misunderstanding of democracy, regretted that their "camp" did not show a similar faith and cohesion.

By 1960 the situation in the United Nations had changed. The democratic principles of pluralism and free competition asserted themselves. Even the Communist world became less monolithic. Communist nations like Yugoslavia, China, Albania, criticized or resisted Moscow's claim for leadership. Nationalism and diversity proved stronger than dogmatic authoritarianism and unity. In the late 1930's, when there was much talk of Fascist international unity and of their unwavering dedication to a common ideal, disunity showed itself even more strongly. Fascism was monolithic only within national boundaries. National Socialist Germany in 1939 did not attack Communist Russia or democratic Britain but semi-Fascist, anti-Communist and antidemocratic Poland which for five years had freely cooperated with Hitler. Fascist Italy attacked in 1940 Greece, ruled by the Fascist dictatorship of General Metaxas. Fascist Spain under Generalissimo Franco followed its self-centered national interests and did not support its much admired and highly praised fellow dictators. In spite of their anti-Communist pact Germany and Japan did not trustfully cooperate. Franco was as much a Fascist as Hitler, but he did not accept Hitler's leadership. Tito and Mao Tse-tung are as much Communists as Khrushchev is, but they follow their own ways and interests.

In the free world the pluralist trends made themselves more strongly felt. The European nations, exhausted or crushed in 1945, regained by 1960 much of their strength and with it their independence. In the same year revolutions in Korea and Turkey overthrew governments, closely allied with, and supported by, the United States without the latter's knowledge or agreement. The trend to "neutralism" grew among nations which the United States had taken for granted as being unconditionally in its "camp." There was a change in the attitude of the United States itself. It insisted less and less on compliance of its allies with its own wishes. It abandoned the oversimplified division of nations into "friends," who do as we please, and "foes" who preserve a critical freedom.

The United States, which until 1947 had been the leading neutralist nation, showed an understanding for the neutralism of others. This new attitude was in line with the principles of the civilization of which the United States had become the bulwark, a civilization opposed to dogmatism, authoritarianism and conformism.

This civilization has demanded new attitudes on the part of its followers, attitudes based upon recognition of equality, first in national life and then in international relations. Domestically it has resulted in its successful though sometimes slow process of education of the citizens toward the recognition of equality—legal, political, and as far as possible also of opportunity—for great and small, rich and poor, highly educated and barely schooled, handsome and deformed alike. The same principles of the recognition of equality underlie the modern Western, not the Fascist or Communist, approach to international relations. These principles are more and more embodied in the structure of the United Nations.

VI

IN THE beginning the United Nations resembled in many ways the League of Nations. It seemed destined to become the instrument of the policies of the great powers. By 1961 the United Nations has turned into something new and different, an organization, the first of its kind, in which all peoples and civilizations meet and discuss world affairs—political, economic, social and cultural—on a footing of equality and according to Western procedure. Instead of welcoming this development, some observers in the democracies appeared troubled by it. They believed that the growing number of member-states might favor Communism. They showed little confidence in the strength of freedom. They were overawed, as they were in the 1930's, by the boasts of totalitarianism. Then some democrats accepted the either-or simplification that there was only a choice between Communism and Fascism. Even today antidemocratic forces outside the Communist world— f.i. Spanish, Portuguese or French traditionalists—conjure up this either-or dilemma, forgetting that Fascism and traditionalism have hardly proven a bulwark against Communism.[6]

[6] Benjamin Welles in The New York Times, July 18, 1961: "What mainly preserves General Franco's grip is his censorship on all fresh ideas. The censor-

In the 1930's, some circles in the West overestimated the chances and power of Fascism and thereby strengthened it. Similarly some circles overestimate today the appeal of Communism. As a result they see the West "losing." But Moscow, though its position has grown immensely stronger as a result of Fascist aggression in 1941, has not always achieved its goals since then. It has failed so far, in spite of much effort, in Austria, Greece, Turkey and Yugoslavia, in Iran, Iraq, Syria and Egypt, in the Congo and generally in Africa, and has made no progress in western Europe, not even in Italy and France. Above all, Moscow was unable to turn the United Nations into an instrument of its policy, and its failure explains the open hostility which Khrushchev has lately shown to United Nations activities and organs. It goes without saying that the United States, too, is unable to use the United Nations as an instrument of its policy. In this case, however, this inability conforms to the principles which underlie the policy of the United States and of the United Nations. The principles of democratic pluralism and the force of nationalism have prevented the United Nations from being dominated by single great powers or power blocs. At the same time these principles create and preserve the pan-human or universal character of the United Nations.

Like every major change in history, the accession of many peoples to nationhood during the last years has created difficult problems. Not only peoples of ancient civilization and fame like the Arabs and Indians have formed independent nations but also the African peoples which truly might be called "young" in the community of nations. Becoming a nation does not set them apart from the older nations but rather acts as a uniting factor. These nascent nations feel, as the Europeans did a century ago, a new liberating sense of being a community striving for common goals. In the age of nationalism peoples no longer accept being objects of history made by others; they wish to feel themselves agents of their own fate. They no longer regard their traditional position as unchangeable. Nationalism endows them with a new energy and

---

ship here keeps the windows and doors sealed to free thought while monotonously repeating. . . . The result after twenty-five years appears to have been to bore and depress the Spanish people into political apathy and to provide a climate in which the Communists alone seem to offer militant resistance."

vitality but it subjects them to the same dangers and temptations to which European nations have been subject and to which they have often succumbed in the age of nationalism. Not better (as they often think) nor worse (as the older nations think) than the older nations, though, of course, different from them and among themselves, the new nations demand admission to the world of history and gain it, for the first time in orderly fashion, through the United Nations, which has become the gateway to participation in global history.

The last chapter in this process is now being written with the admission of so many African peoples or nations-to-be. Their presence, unforeseen in 1945 or even 1955, gives the United Nations a new look. China, India, the Middle East have played throughout the centuries a great role in world history and civilization; Africa south of the Sahara played none. Its entrance into history, understood as the common recorded experience of mankind, coincides with their admission to the United Nations. The transition of the peoples of Europe, Asia and the Americas, to modern nationhood has been a long and painful historical process. Seen in perspective, the transition of the Africans from traditional to modern national society, with all its inherent complexities, is not only progressing rapidly but relatively smoothly. The rise of nationalism in Africa puts the capstone to the growing edifice of mankind. It confirms the dawn of a new era of history. While the African peoples enter for the first time a relationship of equal partnership with the longer established nations of the other continents, they are meeting, also for the first time, among themselves. With them, their national, African and pan-human states of consciousness are developing simultaneously.[7]

[7] The fate of African leaders like Jomo Kenyatta and Patrice Lumumba is beginning to stir Americans of African descent. On April 1, 1961 Jamaicans demonstrated before British Prime Minister Harold Macmillan with banners demanding "Freedom for Kenyatta." The American novelist James Baldwin expressed in *The New York Times Magazine*, March 12, 1961 the universal significance of the Lumumba case: "When the South has trouble with its Negroes, it blames 'outside' agitators and 'Northern' interference. When the nation has trouble with the Northern Negroes, it blames the Kremlin. This is a hazardous thing to do. We give credit to the Communists for attitudes and victories which are not theirs. We make of them champions of the oppressed, and they could not, of course, be more delighted." The young play-

The common African consciousness does not imply African unity or unification, as little as a similar consciousness does in Europe or Latin America. From region to region, interests differ and conflict. Some African frontiers will be hotly disputed among African states, as there have been long and bitter frontier feuds among European and Latin-American nations. Efforts to federate have so far failed in Africa, but they failed equally among Scandinavian or Central American states, though they show a greater affinity among themselves than do the various African regions. What unites Africans today, among themselves and with nations on other continents, is their nationalism. This nationalism makes them reluctant to become junior partners of some great power whose wisdom they do not trust implicitly. Their own judgment may be colored by anticolonial resentment, but it has been pointed out already, that this resentment is hardly as strong as that which European peoples felt against fellow Europeans who ruled over them. The North American settlers were never offended or humiliated by the British; nevertheless a lively anti-British resentment colored American thinking and feeling for many decades after 1783.

Today, all nationalism—in Europe as well as in Africa—has to be tempered by the feeling of pan-human interdependence and the responsibilities which it involves. To an unprecedented degree people are meeting together, in the United Nations, in congresses and conferences, in schools and colleges all over the globe. They learn to understand that they are, and will remain, different. The parochial outlook of nineteenth-century Europe and of Marxism applied its own yardsticks to other civilizations and judged them accordingly. Africans, however, are not like Europeans, only "less developed." They are not "children" who will grow up to maturity. Nor are the Europeans alike among themselves and "equally" developed or mature. The age of pan-humanism cannot disregard the great and beneficial variety of men. Though different, nations have to learn to recognize their equality and to cooperate. Father Abd-el-Jalil spoke of "s'accepter différents et s'aimer complémentaires." Vice President Richard M. Nixon said in Moscow in the

wright Lorraine Hansberry agreed in her letter to the editor (*The New York Times Magazine*, March 26, 1961, p. 4) and wrote: "There is every reason to suppose that Mr. Lumumba will ultimately be universally regarded as the spiritual father of a some day truly unified and independent Congo Republic."

summer of 1959 that our goal should not be a victory over other nations but the victory of the whole of mankind over hunger, misery and disease wherever they are to be found on earth.

The historian of nationalism will remember that in the nineteenth century German and Magyar nationalists protested against granting Slavs or Rumanians full equality in the Hapsburg monarchy. They regarded these peoples as backward and unable to govern themselves. They maintained that they had to be educated, through guidance and weighted forms of representation, for a long time before they could reach maturity. Similar was the attitude of some British toward the Irish or of Poles toward the Ukrainians. National prestige and pride, economic interests and the feeling of cultural superiority involving a "mission," intermingled in this attitude. It survives today in the relationship to Asians, Arabs and Africans. In 1956 rumors were spread that the Egyptians were unable to run the Suez Canal. In 1960 ugly jokes were made about Congolese "cannibals." The "atrocities" and "indignities" the Congolese committed against their former overlords were much inferior in ferocity and number to those inflicted over many decades upon Congolese and other Africans. The treatment of the Africans in the Belgian Congo "must be held primarily responsible for the eruption of racial hatred against the whites throughout the colony and the persistent attitude of latent distrust of the Belgians."[8] The trouble with the Congo was not the grant of national independence but that it came so late, with no preparation at all, and that it was promised by the Belgians in the hope of retaining, under a slight disguise, the former relationship. In spite of the chaos which inevitably followed, the Congolese succeeded, with the support of the United Nations, in laying the foundations of a new nation under the most difficult circumstances in a remarkably short time.

VII

WITH the admission of the new members, the United Nations

[8] Edmund C. Schwarzenbach, *Swiss Review of World Affairs*, Zurich, January, 1961. Most Belgians in the Congo were Flemish and, according to Mr. Schwarzenbach, believed in a "divinely appointed hierarchic order denying the blacks both the right and the possibility of evolution as a matter of principle."

witnessed the shift from the rigidity of bipolarization to a multitude of "blocs," each one (with the exception of the small Communist bloc) subdivided into several groups, the members of which voted independently, and often conflicting among themselves, according to their interests and the questions discussed. A vote against a policy supported by the United States did not mean a vote for the Soviet Union but a disagreement with the United States on a specific issue. Nor did the fact that the United States voted sometimes on the same side as the Soviet Union imply any agreement on fundamentals. The policy of independence followed by the non-Communist states was well defined by the Prime Minister of Tanganyika, Julius Nyerere. Appreciative of his country's educational and cultural association with Britain and the United States, he declared before the National Assembly on June 1, 1961, that "it would be wrong to describe independent Tanganyika's policy as that of neutralism, for the word neutral often carries the connotation of not caring. We do care, passionately, about the development of justice, of wellbeing, and of peace throughout the world. We do care about the rights of man, about the independence and self-determination of nations or groups of nations. We do care about having peace both in Africa and in other parts of the world. On these great issues we cannot be neutral. But although our policy will not be one of passive neutrality it will be independent."

Amid loud applause Mr. Nyerere said that Tanganyika would refuse to be the "lobby fodder" of any Power. "We give notice now that no one will be able to count on an automatic vote from us simply because we are their friends. Nor should any country which feels unfriendly towards us assume that we shall automatically vote on the opposite side to it. We shall not automatically condemn a policy because it is said to be a Communist plot. Nor shall we necessarily oppose a policy because it is described by its opponents as an imperialist intrigue. We shall look at every issue in the light of whether we believe it supports the cause of freedom, of justice, and of peace in the world."[9]

Nyerere's statement came during the debate on a proposal that because of the country's meager resources its diplomatic representation should be limited to the United Nations, London and Wash-

[9] *The Guardian*, Manchester, June 3, 1961.

ington. A suggestion was made to establish no diplomatic mission overseas except at the United Nations. Through the latter, the new nation would be able to participate in history; to the latter, its hopes were directed. The Communists, representing a closed and isolationist society, slight the United Nations on principle; the new nations see it as the strongest guarantee of their independence.

Older and stronger nations are following a similar policy of independence and reserve the right to judge each case on its own merits. Speaking to the Canadian parliament at the beginning of 1961, the Minister of External Affairs, Mr. Howard Green, strongly disagreed with some NATO countries which had demanded that members should always support fellow members, or at least abstain from voting if they thought they could not support the fellow member's position, especially in colonial questions. Mr. Green voiced Canada's determination to vote independently in the United Nations. A similar stand was taken by the newly elected President of Brazil, Janio Quadros, an ardent opponent of Communism. "Far from being erratic or irresponsible the new president simply feels that the time has come for Brazil to play a more important and a more independent role in world affairs. He can be expected to make policy decisions on any given issue strictly in terms of what he thinks is best for his country's interests. . . . [His] new independence in foreign policy is also likely to take much of the wind out of the sails of the opposition which has been calling Quadros a Yankee tool. His program is likely to be one which will cut the ground under the Communists and Castro-like leftist elements."[10]

The most curious aspect of the Brazilian wish for no longer being taken for granted as "lobby fodder" was the apparent necessity to explain to the United States public that this step by a conservative liberal patriot was not an act of Communist opposition to the United States. Quadros established diplomatic and

[10] Robert J. Alexander, "New Look in Brazil," *The New Leader*, March 20, 1961. See also Tad Szulc in *The New York Times*, March 5, 1961: "The most curious aspect of it is that Senhor Quadros is so avowedly anti-Communist that the Communists and leftist ultranationalists violently oppose him in domestic affairs, calling him a tool of the United States, and that his plans for repairing the Brazilian economy are so sensible and conservative as to enchant Brazilian experts and to encourage them in providing aid to him."

economic relations with Communist nations; he pointed out that the United States and Canada maintain similar relations. By establishing friendly relations, he was as little willing to make his country dependent upon Moscow as were Jawaharlal Nehru, President Nasser or President Bourguiba. The last, after sending his envoy to negotiate for Moscow's support against France, declared: "I am not practicing blackmail. I am simply convinced that the Soviet Union can help us because our objectives are similar. We are not satellites or pawns of the West. Whoever wants to help us, can help us. What counts to us, is the welfare of our country." The statesmen of the underdeveloped countries face the difficult task of raising their people to higher levels of welfare and literacy and of eradicating the glaring social and economic inequalities which plague the premodern nations today and which, a few centuries ago, characterized the nations of western and northern Europe, too.[11]

Another difficulty facing the new nations today as it faced the advanced nations in the past, is that of national integration, of fusing different ethnic, religious, social and cultural groups into a high-consensus society. This problem has not always been successfully solved even in advanced nations. On its solution the stability, the progress and even the survival of many Asian, African and Latin-American countries may depend. The task is in the new nations as difficult as it was in the old ones. Pluralistic federalism may overcome many tensions. A British-trained elite in Nigeria, resembling that of India, was determined to master the problem by democratic federalism. "Nigerians are proud that we have attained our independence with a minimum of bitterness and without a revolution that is sanguinary," Dr. Nnamdi Azikiwe, Nigeria's Governor General, declared in Lagos in 1961. "We are dedicated to the task of creating a free and strong nation, enriched by the diversity of language and culture and the variety of social and religious patterns in our country. We strive to make manifest in our daily activities respect for human dignity, firm belief in the rule of law and in the principle of the brotherhood of man."[12]

The lack of integration of the new nations explains the difficulty

[11] Bourguiba, quoted in *The New York Times*, August 4, 1961.
[12] *Federal Nigeria*, vol. IV, 1961, nos. 1–3.

of introducing there Western democratic systems and the rise of one-party or one-man regimes. Again, the new nations are not alone in that situation. Torn by internal dissension and tottering at the brink of civil war, France in 1958 took refuge in a one-man rule, which represented a modernized version of two predemocratic French governmental traditions, seventeenth-century monarchy and nineteenth-century plebiscitary military dictatorship. While resuscitating and preserving the forms of Western parliamentary democracy, Dr. Konrad Adenauer exercised a dictatorial influence integrating the fragments left by the Nazi catastrophe into a workable federal republic and guiding it into an association with the West. One-man regimes and the decisive influence of the armed forces on political life have been familiar for well over a century in many Latin-American nations.

In underdeveloped countries one-man or one-party regimes may fulfill the need of symbols around which the nation can integrate and begin to pursue common objectives. In the elections held by the British in Kenya in February, 1961, Tom Mboya, the leader of the Kenya African National Union, emerged as victor. In spite of the overwhelming democratic endorsement which his party received, Mboya declared on March 10 that in "the initial stages" a one-party government would be "necessary" for the stability and the development of democracy in Kenya. "Danger would come not from traditions or tribalism, but from a struggle for power between the parties. Inevitably this would produce violence and instability." In some countries like Ghana and Tunisia, the cult of personality has become a ritual in politics. In a speech on June 1, 1959, Bourguiba called himself "the sincere and disinterested spokesman of the national conscience" who "has fought for the cause of the people so much and so well that the course of life of the man and the people have been led to merge." No room for public criticism exists in Egypt or Tunisia. They represent a social and national revolution, in which unity and solidarity have gained at the expense of debate and discussion. These dictatorships may be the only way to build the foundation for the development in underdeveloped countries of democratic institutions on a broad basis.[13] Such development is apparently going on in Mexico, which half

[13] See Keith Callard, "The Republic of Bourguiba," *International Journal*, Toronto, Winter 1960/61, and *The Christian Science Monitor*, June 6, 1961.

a century after the revolution continues to be a one-party state ruled by the Party of the Institutionalized Revolution. Until recently the army played the decisive role in the party and the strongest general became president. Since 1946, when General Manuel Avila Camacho left office, civilians have been elected presidents, a fact testifying to the successful growth of a powerful middle class and to the stabilization of Mexican society.

VIII

THE UNITED STATES, absorbed since the late 1940's in an oversimplified view of mankind as caught in a bipolar struggle, tended to accept as welcome allies governments which for their own reasons pursued an anti-Communist policy, even when they did little for the social betterment of their peoples or flaunted antidemocratic principles. In this way a distorted image of the true nature of the United States and of democracy has been created abroad and has weakened and confused the cause of the West.

Too often "democracy" seemed identified not with active popular participation and advance in liberty but with repression and political apathy. An example of such a confusion existed in the minds of young Koreans after more than a decade of close contact with the United States forces. There the regime of Syngman Rhee which was supported by the United States in the name of anti-Communism was accused of widespread corruption and arbitrariness and was overthrown by a students' revolt on April 27, 1960. As a result of free elections John Myun Chang became Prime Minister on August 12, free discussion and a parliamentary regime were introduced, and the new government began to tackle Korea's serious economic problems, caused not only by corruption and inefficiency but also by the growth of population which rapidly overtook the available food supply, by decrease of farm productivity and the rise of farm indebtedness. Impatient for quick reforms and for a higher morality in Korean public life, an officers' junta overthrew Chang's short-lived parliamentary regime less than a year later.

"What is democracy?" an American reporter was asked over and over by Koreans in 1961. "We know what democracy is," said a young colonel, "you showed it to us. It was the Syngman Rhee

regime." An American turned to the colonel and asked in astonish-
ment whether he really believed that the authoritarianism of former President Rhee represented the United States' version of
democracy. The colonel was just as astonished. "Of course," he
said earnestly. "We did not like Rhee, but it was you who supported him all the time and called him a great democrat. That was
your version of democracy." This theme recurs frequently in Seoul.
Americans in the city find to their surprise that some young Koreans picture American democracy not as Americans think of it
but as a reflection of a hated government supported by the United
States.

"Korea is not ready for political democracy. There is too much
to do, too much suffering in the country. We need efficiency,
honesty, dedication, and these will lead some day to free political
rule. In the meantime, the government that supplies these things
is the true supporter of democracy, the real democracy." In one
set of words or another, this is the contention of the young army
officers who gambled their future on the success of the junta. Give
us enough time, they say, and perhaps we can afford the luxury
of democracy. Against these men are the young Koreans who believe that the army officers are simply cloaking a grab for power
in pleasant terms when they speak of democracy. But even the
young people who oppose the junta and helped set off the student
revolution of 1960 are contemptuous of the parliamentary democracy that followed. Among the young Koreans, for the junta or
against it, little good is said these days about the Chang regime.
But steadfastly and passionately many young Koreans, who for the
first time in their lives tasted the joys of free discussion after last
year's revolution, refuse to believe that democracy is impossible for
South Korea.[14]

Another deeply disturbing situation of American military support for an ineffective and corrupt government, put into power and
maintained by American forces, was found in Laos at the end of
1960. An American reporter wrote about this "right-wing government" that it rested upon "the questionable loyalty of most of the
army of about 29,000 men. But the army could cast up more Kong
Les [young patriotic officers eager for reform] tomorrow morning,
for its young officers represent the best educated and, often, the

[14] A. M. Rosenthal in *The New York Times*, July 22, 1961.

most selfless segment of the entire population. They are horrified by the effects of corruption and inefficiency they see all about them, and many could conceivably, like Kong Le, turn to the Left because the Right made it impossible for them to fight the [pro-Communist] Pathet Lao effectively. As a Western diplomat observed to me: 'Kong Le has introduced a new era to Laos, channelling the emotions and aspirations of all discontented non-Communists.' For the first time, the voice of the underprivileged is being heard in Laos. Although regimes may attempt to do so, they will never be able to revert to the previous condition under which the dozen families ruled and all the rest served their feudal lords—albeit in lackadaisical Laotian fashion." Once more, a right-wing military American policy, pursued in disregard of American principles and long-range interests, played into the hands of Communism.[15]

Another example of the devaluation of the values of the modern West is supplied by the recent attitude on the part of the United States government toward Spain's dictatorial regime. American opposition to it should not be simply based on the fact that it represents a one-man rule. Spain may or may not be one of the socially and politically underdeveloped countries where the ways of modern Western civilization cannot (yet) be applied. But the case of Generalissimo Franco's government is different: it openly despises and rejects the modern West. On June 3, 1961, at the formal opening of the Spanish Cortes, Generalissimo Franco launched a scathing attack on Western liberalism, capitalism and democracy, which he declared heading for disaster, whereas he hailed his "organic" democracy as the wave of the future. The speech, "which contained all of the familiar anti-Western strictures of the days when [Franco] supported Nazi Germany and Fascist Italy, was as significant for what it left out as for what it contained." No measures to alleviate the plight of Spain's agricultural workers, no agrarian reforms were announced. Spain's social and economic problems, the glaring maldistribution of wealth, the shutting-out of all modern ideas, continued in spite of the large economic help of more than one billion dollars which the United

[15] Robert S. Elegant in *The New Leader*, January 23, 1961. See also *The Christian Science Monitor*, December 21, 1960, and August 12, 1961.

States provided in addition to military investments. An American correspondent pointed to the danger which this situation involved for the reputation of the United States and its democracy: "The Catholic Church, far more reactionary here than elsewhere, tends to mistrust the United States. . . . Intellectuals and students see Washington as the principal prop for the Caudillo. They begin to identify us with his stultified regime. Unreasonably, some conclude that we prefer to keep Spain underdeveloped and dictatorially controlled."[16]

IX

THE PROBLEMS of national integration, of one-man or one-party rule, of the modernization of the structure of society in the direction of greater equality, are in no way confined to the "new" or ex-colonial nations. Their growth to nationhood and their behavior do not present any difficulties unknown to older nations. The difficult transfer of authority has on the whole (with the exception of a few cases like Algeria) never been accomplished on as vast a scale with relatively so little friction as in the last fifteen years in Asia and Africa. In Europe and the Americas the dissolution of empires was accompanied by much greater strife and bloodshed. The manner in which Sierra Leone, Britain's oldest African colony, achieved independence in 1961, may not be typical but it is not unique. In Freetown, the capital, the Duke of Kent, representing the Queen, handed over to Prime Minister Sir Milton Margai royal instruments recognizing Sierra Leone as an independent nation. At the same time, the independence was celebrated at a special thanksgiving service in St. Paul's cathedral in London, where Dr. R. E. Kelfa Caulka, Sierra Leone's Acting High Commissioner in Britain, read the lesson from the new English Bible in the presence of high British dignitaries.

In practically all cases the transition to independence was smoother than historical experience of former times would have

---

[16] See C. L. Sulzberger, The New York Times, February 9, 1959; Benjamin Welles, ibid., June 5, 1961; and the editorial, ibid., June 6, 1961. The problem of American-Spanish relations is excellently presented by Arthur P. Whitaker, Spain and the Defense of the West. Ally and Liability, published for the Council on Foreign Relations (New York: Harper, 1961).

allowed to expect. Modern Western civilization showed an equal resourcefulness in the solution of its colonial problem as it had done in the solution of its social problem, the relationship of capital and labor. In both cases, it has taught the underpriviliged to aspire to equality and human dignity. Thereby it paved the way to a new interpersonal and international relationship, based upon the emancipatory message which has characterized Western civilization since the seventeenth century, first in a national framework and then on a global stage.

In the 1960's many Western developments are converging. Mankind enters the age of pan-nationalism, which has its roots in the social-political development of the modern West. At one and the same time mankind faces the threat of nuclear weapons, first conceived by the science of the modern West, and the promise of pan-humanism, of a world order based on law, a hope which has grown throughout the history of modern Western thought. The fateful half-century from 1910 to 1960 appears in retrospect as the transition from the relatively balanced Europe-centered world of the nineteenth century to a new global order. The central event of this transitional period was the disintegration of the British Empire and the totalitarian attack upon its liberal foundations.

The nineteenth century was the era of the *Pax Britannica*. "British leadership was characterized by caution, insistence on a legal basis for intervention, use of persuasion rather than force, preference for economic pressures if force was used, and reluctance to assume general responsibilities. Taken as a whole, British power proved adequate to organize the Empire with a quarter of the world's population as an increasingly free union of [territories] in various stages of evolution toward independence in the spirit of the common law; to organize Europe with another quarter of the world's population as a balance of power controlled by British policy operating through the Concert of Europe so effectively that the peace was only occasionally broken by relatively localized wars; to organize the world outside Europe and the Empire as a body of independent states in varying degrees of dependence upon British finance and naval control sufficient to keep wars localized; and to organize commerce everywhere according to the system of freedom of enterprise, freedom of trade and freedom of capital movement, thus relieving political frontiers of the severe strain to which they would be subjected if they constituted also impassable economic frontiers."[17]

British leadership declined when technology overcame the barriers of distance and the spread of democracy and nationalism began to equalize society. British inability to prevent the war of 1914 pointed to the necessity for change. The most liberal attempt ever conceived to order the world on the basis of inequality had failed. "The world has to be done all over again on a new basis and on an enormous scale," Jan C. Smuts wrote in 1918. "Europe is being liquidated, and the league of nations must be the heir to the great estate. . . . Surely the only statesmanlike course is to make the league of nations the reversionary in the broadest sense of these empires. In this debacle of the old Europe, the league of nations is no longer an outsider or stranger, but the natural master of the house. It becomes naturally and obviously the solvent for a problem which no other means will solve."[18]

The members of such a league must agree on procedures rather than on matters of substance, and must begin to identify their aspirations and means with the functioning of the world order. "Constitutional government," Quincy Wright wrote in 1942, "consists in a determination of the citizens of the state that adherence to the procedures set forth in the constitution shall be treated as more important than any specific grievance, demand or reform. Until the people of the world are similarly determined to place procedures ahead of substance, we may expect . . . little respite from wars and rumors of wars." Peace can be assured by constitutional procedures in an international organization. "Today such an organization must embrace the world and must be able to adjust rapidly changing opinions and rapidly changing conditions to each other if there is to be enduring peace."

Such an organization began to emerge in the 1960's. It is no longer dominated by one great power or by the confrontation of superpowers. In a book written during World War II, Robert Strausz-Hupé argued that the independence and freedom of as-

[17] Quincy Wright, "The Historic Circumstances of Enduring Peace," Annual Report of the American Historical Association for 1942, vol. III (Washington: Government Printing Office, 1944), pp. 361 ff.

[18] J. C. Smuts, The League of Nations. A Practical Suggestion (London: Hodder & Stoughton, 1918), pp. 11 ff.

sociation of small nations are essential features of a world system adaptable enough to allow for change. The existence of the small nations imposes self-restraint upon the great powers. "And self-restraint is the leaven of international collaboration as it is of a free society." In this brilliant formulation the essence of modern Western civilization is well summed up. In the interest of a world order of freedom the primary objective to which the United States should commit itself after the war, Strausz-Hupé wrote, "is the survival and reinvigoration of Western civilization. . . . The concept of the West is not an exclusive concept. . . . Western integration and world integration are not mutually exclusive goals."[19]

A reinvigorated modern Western civilization can become the cornerstone of a world order based upon freedom, diversity and tolerance, the matrix of pan-nationalism and pan-humanism. The North Atlantic Community can serve this goal only if it resolutely sheds the last vestiges of the colonial order and refuses to be an association of the "haves" who think above all of defending their privileges. In a book dealing with the problems of NATO, André Fontaine has stressed the need for a psychological reorientation of its attitudes and goals. "First of all," he wrote, "it is of prime importance that NATO should stop thinking that it is an end in itself and that it merits some kind of eternity. Its aim should be peace, or at least an armistice in a cold war to which no human being can resign himself and the absurdity of which we should ceaselessly denounce.

"NATO must, therefore, rise to the occasion and face its responsibility. . . . It must work up a tireless campaign for world reconciliation in every possible circumstance—at the United Nations, in international conferences, everywhere, as Mr. Nixon did during his visit to the Soviet Union. On every possible occasion it must repeat that man's task in this second half of the twentieth century is, first and foremost, to save the human race from the thousand and one things which menace it: war, slavery, hunger, sickness, poverty, illiteracy. NATO must constantly invite the other nations, particularly those belonging to the 'Socialist camp'

[19] "Sombre invocations of Western solidarity against the hordes of Asia are apt to produce a psychosis in which fear is the strongest element." Robert Strausz-Hupé, *The Balance of Tomorrow. Power and Foreign Policy in the United States* (New York: Putnam, 1945), pp. 271–75.

to join it in putting into operation a program which can only succeed on a planetary scale. It should emphasize its desire to hand over responsibility for collective security to the United Nations as soon as it is possible to end the present conflict, which implies, of course, general and controlled disarmament, a Security Council worthy of the name and an international police force. NATO must continually push to the fore plans with these objectives."[20]

Western civilization and Europe almost destroyed themselves in allowing, in their midst, the triumph of Fascism and of a self-centered traditionalist nationalism. The victory of 1945 saved Western civilization and a large part of Europe. It made manifest the revolutionary transformation which had gone unnoticed for several decades. Two new facts arose out of this situation. The threat of wars among European nations (f.i. France and Germany) disappeared from the horizon. Old national jealousies lost their intensity. Cooperation in a European community became possible. At the same time the peoples of Asia and Africa emerged into equal partnership in world history. The North Atlantic Community and the United Nations are the very imperfect symbols of these two simultaneous transformations. It takes time for the mind of man to adapt itself to such fundamental changes. For the historian looking back to the not distant past it is astonishing that the Atlantic Community and the United Nations exist at all and that they have made, in a short time, as much progress as they did.

X

IN THE first era of global history, an era fraught with great dangers and greater promises, three considerations should guide the conduct of those countries which thanks to their ideas and their power are primarily responsible for the course of international cooperation. The first consideration concerns the relationship of great powers and weaker nations. A North American historian, defining the relationship between his country of birth (Canada) and

[20] André Fontaine, *L'Alliance Atlantique à l'heure du dégel* (Paris: Calman-Lévy, 1960). This book received the Prix Atlantique by the Association Française pour la Communauté Atlantique. See also *Valeurs de base de la Communauté Atlantique*, ed. by the Conference sur la Communauté Atlantique in Bruges (Leyden, The Netherlands: A. W. Sythoff, 1961).

his country of adoption (the United States), pointed out that "no great power seems habitually to be tender, imaginative, or subtle toward a weaker one, even when it is a neighbor. It is true, on the other hand, that the weaker powers are endlessly sensitive, subtle and imaginative toward their overpowering neighbors. . . . Canada had always had to fear the expansive energies of the United States, whether in the overt forms of national and filibustering invasions, or in the peacetime pressure of [economic policy and] dollar diplomacy." A small nation is oversensitive when collaborating with a great power for fear lest collaboration open the way to dominance. This is as true of Canada as of younger, less developed and therefore more distrustful countries.[21]

The second consideration concerns the "cold war," which Communism started in 1917 and which the bipolarized world situation of 1945 so greatly intensified. The tension underlying the cold war will last for a long time to come, perhaps until new power constellations will arise through the growth and cooperation of less committed nations and thereby reduce the cold war to the proportion of before 1945. Communism, which originally denied the trend of nationalism, will discover that nationalism, if it is supported by the broad and willing consent of an awakened population and if it looks to the United Nations for its security, will act as a powerful impediment to attempts at global control. In the years which will have to pass before Communism will learn the lesson of the diversity of mankind and of the strength of the appeal of freedom, the peoples of the North Atlantic Community will have to learn to live with the unresolved problems of the cold war. They will have to exercise the virtues which Plato recognized and St. Augustine accepted as fundamental—prudence, fortitude, moderation and justice. To them should be added three more virtues—patience, the ability of taking a long-range view, and the rejection of a feeling of self-righteousness. Struggle and aggressiveness are essential elements of totalitarianism; moderation

[21] J. Bartlet Brebner, "Persistent Problems in Canadian-American Relations," *Annual Report of the American Historical Association for 1942*, op. cit., pp. 197 ff. Prof. Reginald G. Trotter of Toronto asked the Americans, in order to understand the emotional elements in Canadian attitudes toward the United States, to examine their own traditional attitude toward Britain. *Ibid.*, pp. 205 ff.

and the willingness to see more than one side of an argument are those of modern Western civilization. The West will have to practice these virtues which are rooted in its traditions. On them its leadership of the developing global unity will depend.

The third consideration is a compassionate but never condescending sympathy with those peoples who enter the era of pan-nationalism and pan-humanism, whether they acknowledge it or not, under the inspiration of the modern West. For them it is a rise in status which they enthusiastically embrace in spite of the inherent risks. They refuse to be admonished of these risks by self-appointed paternalistic guardians. Language which implies either a superiority feeling or wishes to subordinate their aspirations to the needs of the great power struggle, will be deeply resented. A better future for the West and for mankind depends on the West's living up to its own principles. The often heard observation that the smaller or underdeveloped peoples respect only force is not only a denial of Western civilization, it is intrinsically false. Such *Machtpolitik* may lead to temporary successes, but in the end it defeats itself.

In the age of Enlightenment the modern West started those developments which led to the growth of nationalism everywhere and to the global intercourse of civilizations. With an open mind the eighteenth century began to establish cultural contacts with China and India, Russia and Islam. In the twentieth century the age of pan-nationalism is merging into the age of pan-humanism. Though the future is unknown, there is no reason for viewing it with pessimism. The problems ahead are new and there are no precedents to guide us. Westerners, having lived in one generation through the horrors of two great wars, of Fascism and Communism, incline to pessimism and melancholic regret. They know that the dominant and apparently secure position which their ancestors enjoyed is passing. But the vast majority of men are today looking forward to a life of greater dignity, to a more human existence than their parents or grandparents have ever known.

The 1960's are not a period of intellectual and spiritual sterility. Great works of art may not be created at present, but the treasures of many centuries in poetry, music and painting are today far more accessible to greater multitudes than they were in the past. Science, including medicine, is progressing more rapidly than in any age before. Dr. Alan T. Waterman, a physicist who has been director of the National Science Foundation in Washington since 1951, told the American Association for the Advance of Science in 1960 that "science is now bringing in discoveries of graver and graver social significance. This trend is bound to continue and indeed to accelerate. Whether future developments take the form of stupendous power over nature's resources, of influence and control over life or over men's minds, or of traffic with our sister planets, they will in all probability raise problems of such concern to the human race that mankind must—repeat must—learn to cooperate in their solution."

The rapid progress of science will not only change our knowledge and mastery of the outside world; it will refine and broaden our concern with our fellow men; it will alter and improve the scope and methods of human welfare and psychological understanding. In the 1960's, men are pushing forward, beyond any previous experience, toward higher forms of international integration—in an Inter-American Alliance for Progress, in Asian and African unity conferences, in the European Common Market, in the North Atlantic Community, in the United Nations. No one foresaw these developments in 1940. They are experiments in building new frameworks for coexistence and cooperation, for mastering problems on the solution of which the survival of great parts of mankind may depend. They respond to real and vital needs and come at a unique opportunity in history. They testify to the creative resourcefulness of the human mind. In them the age of pan-humanism, which the dynamism of modern Western civilization has brought about, takes form as the first era of global history.

Index